What Time Is It?

May God grant you wisdom
and Vision through the thoughts
and ideas in this book.

Blessings

Rev Joe

Table of Contents

Forward

You have purchased or been given this book. If you purchased it, you have set yourself apart from the average. You are interested in change. You are interested in ideas. If you were given this book, someone believes in you and your ability to process such information. That means that whether, or not, you have discovered it, you are above average.

You may find this book to be a challenge in the way it is presented. I hope not too much, or I have failed in my objective to communicate these ideas. However, I do intend to stretch people in their thinking. So . . . ponder concepts and apply principles. This book will be a catalyst to those who find it challenging and a connection to those who find it confirming.

This book is different. This book comes from the core belief that the Bible is the Owner's Manual of life. We are designed and signed by God and we excel at who we are based on our adherence to His instructions for function and purpose. I have endeavored to show Biblical examples along with historical examples because even though times change, the condition of the human spirit, and soul does not. The 20th Century demonstrated that technology and education will only make us more prolific in our vices without some core restraining entity (God) and ethic (the Gospel of Jesus Christ).

I want to state plainly that this book is not a doctrinal treatise. You who hope it is for the sake of lauding or rejecting it are destined to be disappointed. The book is intended to be a three-tiered look at life and living it. May it stand on those merits.

This book is "process targeted" and therefore invests a sizeable segment on the topic of preparation. Necessity dictates it to be so. Some ideas overlap as they reconnect with a particular topic or concept. It is my hope that the different observation points of a particular idea will help confirm its priority.

Finally, it is my prayer that this book will go beyond instruction and will help with rescue and recovery. May God grant it so.

Rev. Joseph Cottle

With heartfelt gratitude, I mention some people by name or by group. Particular thanks to Pamela Miller for taking on the ungainly task of editing this project. It is no small task to take on something that has interjections of vernacular and my tendency toward complex sentences. The use of the colon and its kid brother – the semi-colon – are lost on many modern writers but I chose to invite both to this literary luncheon; she managed to abide their challenging company and leave my book intact.

I must acknowledge my friends at Radical Impact Ministries who have encouraged me to write all this down. You are too numerous to name and some of you wouldn't want to be; so, I thank you as a group. You know who you are. Your loyalty to my place in the Kingdom of God has amazed me and held me together many times when all else was in disarray.

And most significant, my family and my wife in particular, who have waited many years for me to accomplish completing this book, thank you.

I would like to dedicate this book to my father, Rev. Robert Cottle, who was one of my greatest examples of trying to perceive each season of life and prepare ahead of that season to maximize its potential. No one is perfect at such things but in his life, I can point to several seasons that he evaluated before they were fully engaged and the significant adjustments that he made to mitigate hazards and maximize the harvest of each season. His 50 years of small-church ministry, marked with what some would call successes and failures, were years of deep prayer and discernment for the task at hand and what the hidden particulars of the season offered in benefit or deficit to the task. In all, he has been a great example of living for God and good in every season. Thanks, Dad, for the great example. I am forever in debt.

Segment 1

A Great Question

A Great Solution

A Great Revelation

Chapter 1

The Great Question

What Time Is It?

"What time is it?" I asked the small group of teenagers and early-twenty-somethings who attended our Thursday-night leadership meeting. The answers that were shouted back at me ranged from the technically accurate to the sarcastic to the abstract to the philosophical.

"It's 7:45p.m." said the attentive one with the watch.

"Yes, but what time is it?" I asked again.

"It's Thursday evening," said one tall young lady hoping for a quick resolution to so simple a question.

"O.K. but what time is it?" I persisted.

4

"It is 7:45p.m. Thursday, April 14, 2006!" came the response of someone who hoped that compiling all the accurate data would solve the question that was now pushing them to perplexity.

"All very true," I replied again, "but what

time is it really?" Now the more impatient attendees became annoyed.

"Time for you to buy a watch!!" one of the more sarcastic young men comically shot at me. I laughed, being one of those long removed from the habit of wearing a time-piece and retorted that I had heard that many times before. Now my more devoted members ventured to come to my rescue and to solve the crisis of an unsatisfied instructor.

"Spring-time!" ventured a farmer's son to whom it had specific implications.

"Time for battle!" exclaimed one who had just returned from a conference where they were motivated to join the ranks of those fighting the ill effects of media and politics on the culture."

"We're getting closer." I encouraged.

"It's time for Jesus!" emphasized the deeply spiritual young man who had taken several short-term mission trips. Then from among the various shouts and comments I heard him. The devout young man in the back, engaged in the difficult struggle of overcoming less than positive family legacies and a difficult home life.

"The time is NOW!!"

That is what I had been looking for. Now is the only time we have.

We don't have yesterday; it is history. It is only viewable through the window of memory and we have no other access to its pageantry. Yesterday will not be re-written and it will not be de-written. Only with today's writing can we mitigate the implications of yesterday because of its irrevocability. We don't have tomorrow; it is far and away one of the most fragile ideas ever considered in the universe – and it is only an idea. It has no constitution whatsoever without its necessary connection to yesterday and today.

"What time is it?" happens to be one of the most important questions of any situation we find ourselves in. Humorously, who can forget the line from the naughty little ditty in "The Music Man[2]," where con-man, Professor Harold Hill, sings that he is looking for "the girl who knows what time it is". More seriously, we are cautioned of this grave importance from the scene in "Sergeant York[1]," where they have synchronized their watches in the trenches but not with the artillery and at 0610 hour they come up out of the trenches to attack only to have their own artillery shells come raining down on their advance.

This question identifies so many things for us. If it is 7:30 in the evening, we know that the 5:00 crowd will have gone home; the downtown shops will be closed; our friends will have eaten dinner; and the vacuum sweeper and life-insurance salesmen will be making their presentations. The rush hour traffic will have thinned out.

If we need something, we need to know what time it is. If we are doing something, we need to know what time it is. This question is paramount in situations from baking to banking; from touring to taxes; from fishing to flying. Without answering the question, **"What time is it?"** we will not find ourselves being punctual, prescient, and powerful.

Be Punctual, Be Prescient, Be Powerful

Being **punctual** is very important. God has many miracles of convergence for us through which He will provide. In the scriptures we see many encounters with Jesus that were about people being in the right place at the right time. Zacchaeus' determination to be in the right place at the right time won him dinner with the Savior (Luke 19). The Samaritan woman was at the well at precisely the correct moment for her miracle (John 4). Abigail made a timely intersection with David and was able to save her household and secure her future to be known as David's wife instead of Nabal's widow (1st Samuel 25).

Being **prescient** carries a different level of importance. Our events, encounters, and contributions need to be relevant. If we don't know what time it is in terms of culture and circumstance, we will attend, engage and contribute where there is no connection and won't be received. Again, the Bible paints very poignant pictures for us. The Amalekite who claimed to have killed King Saul didn't know what time it was as he stood in front of future-king David; it was no time to brag and it cost him his life (2 Samuel 1).

Modern history also gives us some stark examples: In World War II, Hitler squandered the effective mass of his home-front troops on the Battle of the Bulge with very little consideration of the facts. The "slow to attack or retreat" Montgomery to the North, the "very methodical" Bradley in the center, and the "dashing, daring, and explosively mobile" Patton to the south, made for a combination to which no well-informed leader would expose troops in a bulge situation. Further, the Allied troops now had the experience of the hedgerow fighting to help them destroy German armor.

As well, the Allies were of stronger internal constitution than was known. Not enough of them panicked to make the offensive, effective. Not being prescient left Hitler's enemies – Eisenhower and Patton – smiling, his own field commanders annoyed or exasperated, and the infantry men and German nation devastated.

Being **powerful** has to do with being effective within the scope of our purpose. If we attempt something grand but the timing is wrong we will find some laughing at us, some annoyed with us, and some damaged by us. In Sergeant York's[1] case, the artillery made the gross error of shelling its own troops because it did not know what time it was. Was it powerful? The shell carried the same deadly potential but landed on the wrong army. The artillery had an assignment to make a powerful contribution to the battle for their own side; instead they were negatively powerful as they destroyed their own troops.

The Past – Singing Angel or Haunting Ghost

Not only does the question beg information from the present, it also calls on the past. The question of what time it is now can only be answered in the context of the past. The past tells us what has been gained and what has been lost. The past tells us what has come and gone. The past tells us what has come that is not gone yet and is still at work. The past explains the tracks that mark the landscape of our present, the deep and challenging ruts of habit that nearly break the function of our lives, as we try to get free from or cross over them.

Why are the ruts of habit so hard to escape? God has ordained sowing and reaping as laws governing the activities of this world. Those laws demand a justice that is inescapable. When we are questioning what time it is now, due to sudden and supposedly unforeseen events, we can gain much in the way of understanding current events by looking at what was sown yesterday and in the previous seasons of our past.

When people cry out against the circumstance they find themselves in, they would do better to spend a little time in review to see what they planted in the preceding days. Today – the time that it actually is - should have few surprises; and has very few surprises, for those who are properly processing the past.

So then, the past can be friend or foe. The past may be a sweet singing angel to you or may be a haunting ghost. When you lie down, does the past come and sing you to sleep with the accomplishments of the day, or does he continually repeat failures and omissions. He only knows one line, "This is what has been! This is what has been!" Does that line bring you comfort, or does it steal your joy and your peace?

If the past is to you a haunting ghost, what is he saying that you don't wish to hear? Is he telling you about the deeds you've done and how they have fallen below the pale of acceptable behavior, how they have hurt other people, how they have hurt you; or is he telling you about deeds you did not do that you should have and how those omissions have brought about your failures and the failures of others. Maybe he is telling you about the deeds of some other person that affected you, that you were a victim of, and that is how he haunts you. (By the way, just because he repeats this stuff from the past does not mean that he is helping you process it properly).

How do you deal with him? Are you simply trying to silence him? Many see silencing as the only answer for the Ghost of the past and therefore go about their life trying to drown out the sound of his voice. One of these methods is the great blind and dead-end ally of substance abuse. There are those who are simply after the "high". They may be the easiest to recover. There are those who have a genetic or chemical weakness. They are quite difficult to recover. However, the person who is using substance abuse as a coping mechanism may be the most difficult because when this is combined with the first two reasons for substance abuse, the chains and fetters are almost too difficult to break.

Many people are trying to hide from the ghost of the past in the world of fantasy. It has been said that the great addiction of this generation is fantasy. And, there we find people completely obsessed with video games, pornography, soap-operas, pro-sports and many other things, attempting (often subconsciously) to get far enough into their fantasy that the voice of their own progressing history will fade. It is one of the great delusions of our day.

Often, people just try to ignore him by continuing to do the ineffective things they have always done, only doing them louder, faster, more often, with more pomp and ceremony, or with more resignation to duty. The great deception of this is that this leads to a glorification of our excuses for the behavior until we have made our compensative faults into a fortress of behavior that prevents us from seeing the outside world effectively and prevents anyone else from coming in to our fortress and helping us.

Most suicides are an effort to silence the ghost of the past. He is not the conduit of hope to many people. He can be incorrigibly cold about his recitations, showing no sense for assessment, or timing, or even whole truths. People begin to believe that the ghost of the past is the prophet of the future, and they see no way to mitigate his grave and repetitive message. They make a dreadfully wrong assessment of the ghost's narrations, an even worse assessment of the future, and finally a catastrophic decision of how to deal with it all.

Now, what of the prophetic implications of the ghost of the past? If the substance abusers, the delusional, and the suicidal are not at least some-what correct in their assessment of the prophetic nature of the past, then what is correct? The past is quite a prophet. He has lost very few. His prophecy of the future (by quoting the past) is as sure as any prophecy has ever been. The ghost of the past will become tomorrow's frightening, unrestrained and unrelenting monster of consequence except for one thing – **today.**

It is interesting how daunting the monster of consequences, the monster known as "tomorrow" appears, when in truth, he is the most wispy, flimsy, "blown away with one-word exhale," imposter. Yes, he is an imposter! **Tomorrow is the most fragile idea ever considered in the universe.** What makes him so fragile? What can stop a monster with all the appearance of unrelenting consequence? *Today!!*

Chapter 2

The Immediate Solution

Today

Weapon Against the Past and the Future

Today is our weapon against the siege of the past. Today is the way that we exorcize this ghost. Today is the weapon with which we vanquish the monster of consequences named "tomorrow". Today has the potential for transformation of the ghost of the past from specter to angel and the monster of tomorrow into a benevolent friend. The next five minutes may be more important to your peaceful sleep than the previous 168 hours that comprise a week's worth of history. If we would only realize that having the next five minutes means that we have repentance, redemption, reconciliation, restoration, available to us.

Most of us blow our "today's" making excuses for the past to save our pride and our self-concept that are based on the shouting of the past that we don't like. If we would just give up our pride and self-concept we might find that we can

accomplish some things that legitimize a proper sense of pride, and build for us a new and more favorable self-concept. We spend too much time and energy trying to demonstrate to others that we have "reasons" for the ugly story the past keeps telling. **The same amount of time and energy targeted productively, will generally propel us far enough down the road to accomplishment that we neither have time nor necessity to explain the past.**

Today is not to be squandered like yesterday. Yesterday's excuses and reasons have proven to be insufficient in the test of effectiveness for progress. Another day of drunkenness, of fantasy, of gossiping, bullying, finger-pointing, of lethargy and dormancy, of hibernation, will only perpetuate the song the Ghost of the Past is singing and deepen the ruts that keep us from steering our lives out of dysfunctions like poverty, addiction, broken promises, and broken relationships. "Today is the day of salvation," the Apostle tells us, but the full impact of that statement is found when we understand that TODAY is the ONLY day of salvation!

It really doesn't matter that yesterday we were one thing or another, or that tomorrow we intend to stop being one thing or another. Yesterday has slipped from the pliability of our grasp into the granite of history. Tomorrow is an elusive imagination that, at best, exists in our faith—faith which requires today's action to give it any authenticity.

We need to take the next five minutes and use it redemptively. Make a phone call and apologize. Sit down and journal your prescient thoughts. Go clean the sink. Go comb the dog. Go fly the kite. For heaven's sake (and your own) get up and do something! Break free from this dreadful morass of sitting and sulking about what might have been, about what someone else should have provided, about what you deserve, about what the lottery could bring you, about your desire to sit there sulking. GET UP AND MOVE. Jesus said, "Take up your bed and walk!"

Chapter 3

The Great Revelation

Seasons - Windows of Optimization

So, how do I understand what time it is? Is there a way to categorize the time that it "actually" is so that I can appropriately respond? Yes, there is. God has instructed us through His great wise-man Solomon that time is made up of seasons. Listen to Ecclesiastes 3:1 "To everything there is a season, a time for every purpose under heaven."

"What are seasons then?" one might ask. "And would the author please stop playing word games?"

Seasons are windows of optimization. Life is made up of many of these seasons. There is a best time to do any certain thing and finding that best time is one of the secrets to successful, effective, efficient living. If one can determine the appropriate activity for the season, there is an exponentially greater chance for success.

"While the earth remains, Seedtime and harvest, Cold and heat, Winter and summer, And day and night Shall not cease." (Genesis 8:22)

The law of sowing and reaping is God's proclamation of the function of the earth. We must begin our consideration with this law in mind. This law compels us to ask the question, "What do I want to harvest at the end of this season or in the next season?" which must be answered before we have any hope of the proper use of our season.

Every season is a preparation for the next. If we blow one season we are out of sync with the next season. If we blow two seasons, we are at a timing deficit that will make proper harvest almost impossible. If we blow three or four seasons, we can only stand and look at a harvest to which we have no access.

For many years I have observed and compared people's lives including my own. I have wondered what is the difference between the successful-happy, the successful-miserable, those who don't appear to be successful and yet are happy and those whose lack of success causes them no small anxiety and frustration? Of the many reasons and theories that many wise-men, theologians and psychologists have offered, I have observed that the people who do things in season, who do things with very accurate timing are the happy ones, even if they don't yet appear to have achieved success.

I have watched the people who do things with no sense of timing and are perpetually out of season. They live grossly frustrated and often catastrophic lives. They attempt to do things in disregard of the optimum windows for the particular activity or venture, and experience drastic consequences. Their lives become a jumbled confusion of competing and often contrary dreams and goals, responsibilities and recreations, courses and consequences. There is no recovery until they stop, make a proper assessment of their season and begin to operate within its windows of optimization. So then let's consider some of these optimums.

Segment 2

Seasons of Optimum Preparation

The Foundation

For the building and living of your life, you are the foundation on which all things stand. If you fall, your plans and projects fall. Your personhood or the multifaceted construction of who you are, who you are becoming, will be the deciding factor in whether or not your dreams can stand up to their own fulfillment. Will you have enough strength of body, strength of character, strength of soul, strength of Spirit? Will your faith in God be the rock on which your foundation stands and produce when natural means are bending and breaking?

This foundation of your personhood is the most important preparation you can possibly ever accomplish. It is so important it never really ends; and yet there is certainly an optimum window for preparing the person. That window would be before a direction or assignment is engaged.

Chapter 4

What is Relevant?

It is very important to keep up with our seasons. So, let's look at that idea positively. Primary school prepares us for middle school which prepares us for high school which prepares us for college which prepares us for career. That is the proper way to experience and process each season: living the present and preparing for the future. Good living is prepared living and therefore, good living must be preparatory living.

Humorously, I have observed (my mother has a theory that involves the word "participation", but she is not writing this book) the way in which primary school prepares some of us for high school, and high school prepares some of us for college, and college prepares some of us for careers. There are the under achievers and their victims…

<u>Distracted male</u>: "Psst, Billy, look out the window! That squirrel just picked his nose."

<u>Billy</u>: "So did you, but the squirrel knew what to do with it. Shut up! I can't hear!"

<u>Distracted female</u>: "Psst, Veronica, look at those shoes Jennifer wore, and with those shorts! I'd rather wear Go-Go boots than those things!"

<u>Veronica</u>: "You are wearing Go-Go boots. Shut-up and study!

There are the mediocre achievers and their victims (mostly teachers) …

<u>Apathetic male</u>: "Mr. Bunson, I didn't know what to do for a science project until I found these mushrooms growing on this deteriorating sock in the locker room. I thought the green fumes were note-worthy.

<u>Mr. Bunson</u>: "Aaackk! Put it in the sealed terrarium. You get a - GAAGGG! - D+. Now where's that number to the Area 51 Containment Team."

There are the over achievers and their victims…

<u>Female over-achiever</u>: Ms. Participle, this is my term paper on Shakespearian influence over the "Angry Love" culture and others who read his Sonnets. It is 85 pages written on Icelandic papyrus with Byzantine ink stored 1552 years in the bottom of a monastery.

<u>Ms. Participle</u>: Wonderful Monique. You get an "A". (And everyone else gets a "C- ".)

I don't know if there was really any difference except that the smart kids got better help from their parents or older brothers and sisters; with siblings, blackmail is power and good grades.

Seriously, some wonder what the advantage is of studying hard and excelling in primary education. I watched four kids at one graduation walk off with as much as $80,000 in non-sports scholarships!

So now, let's take the example apart negatively: if we mess up the college season by quitting before the degree is issued, we will experience some deficit or difficulty in fully accessing/harvesting the career. If we mess up the high school season by quitting early (really dumb), or even just goofing off (trying to look cool while being dumb) and squandering the learning opportunity, we can't properly access – if at all – the college we need for that career.

College entrance counselor: "What did you say your GPA was? Hmmmm, that puts you somewhere between dragonflies and hoofed mammals. Give me your tuition money and head over to the laboratory warehouse . . ."

Now the career is for the most part out of reach. If we mess up the primary education, a degreed field is excluded from consideration and something must be found that requires no more than basic writing and arithmetic skills.

Temp-service recruiter: "When you get to Acme Computers, ask for Charley. He has your push-broom. Oh, and he said, 'Don't touch nothing.'

If reading and writing are missing, there is a lightning strike's chance of having a "successful" economic future of any kind (try marrying well).

<u>You, to a total stranger at a beach-party of drunken hooligans</u>:
"How rich did you say your daddy is?"

**** There is no such thing as luck!! There is only the occasion where a specific level of preparedness meets with opportunity or disaster!!****

The idea is too prescient to the times to leave. Consider the state of marriage in this context of preparation. Many (if not most) marriages break up from lack of preparation. People haven't prepared financially, they haven't prepared physically, they haven't prepared emotionally, they haven't prepared spiritually and when they enter into what the Scriptures call a "one flesh" relationship, the oneness is fragmented and incomplete.

They offer a "less than prepared" gift physically, thinking that "love" will make up for it or that the marriage boundaries will take care of themselves without maintenance. Then when their health crashes or their partner finds out that they don't really respect themselves or their partner enough to maintain themselves, the partner disconnects – and they are surprised.

Maybe they aren't prepared financially. They don't know how to keep a check-book or have no control over credit. They don't know how to say "No" to themselves. Sooner or later (and sooner rather than later) the bottom falls out of that kind of living and the crisis is too much to bear. ("Honey, the bank president showed up at the shoe-store today with a swat team and took my debit card. It wasn't even close to the expiration date. Hold me.") Once again there is surprise when there shouldn't be.

Often, they are not prepared emotionally. Now, some ask the question, "How can anyone be emotionally prepared for marriage?" That question implies that there is so much change and adjustment that no one is adequately prepared. That is only partially true. We may not be "prepared" in the sense that there is no adjustment necessary, but we can be "prepared" by being emotionally well or whole before we get married. This is one of the most overlooked preparations in the marriage preparedness question.

People come to marriage without healing from past wounds and they mistakenly believe that if the other person completes them, they will heal or hide those wounds. The truth is that marriage, with its adjustments, exposes and amplifies those wounds and the bad coping mechanisms that have prevented their healing for so long. Often the spouse is bewildered by them, or if pre-informed is frustrated by the fact that they, as a spouse, are not adequate to the task of healing this person they love.

Take this emotional un-preparedness to the second marriage and you will quickly understand why the statistics for second marriages are so much worse than first marriages. Not only do they have the unresolved issues that broke up the first marriage, that first marriage is now another unresolved issue. They didn't take the time between first and second marriage to properly assess the causes of the first marriage failure, and now they have added to those causes a new issue for the next marriage.

Chapter 5

The Scriptures' View of Preparation

The scripture has many examples of this season and its processes. Genesis 39-43 tell us the story of Joseph and his season of preparation before he ascended to the management of Egypt. He learned domestic management in the house of Jacob. He perfected that skill in Potiphar's house and added to it knowledge of protocol. He learned corporate management in the Egyptian prison system and after all that preparation, ascended to second in command in the kingdom.

Joseph's "Season of Preparation" was extensive, arduous, humbling, even demeaning, sometimes unjust. Yet it was also targeted to specifics, exhaustive, comprehensive. When it finally passed into the season of promotion, the promotion was as comprehensively good as the preparation had been difficult. His original vision had been of his brothers bowing before him. As Daddy's favorite, he expected that to be enforced by Daddy on the family ranch, but his destiny was so much greater than that. He could have achieved promotion on the ranch with minimal preparation, but the office God had appointed for him was so much greater and therefore the window of preparation was also greater.

Consider Moses in Exodus 1-3. How was God going to produce a leader for his people when the pool of talent was a pool of slaves? No one was in leadership. No one had the autonomy to learn. So, God used his very enemies to train the man that would lead his people. It should be noted that God started some 80 years ahead of the day of deliverance. He chose parents that had enough faith in God to hide their baby from Pharaoh's death squads. He then chose Pharaoh's own daughter to bring the child into the palace. And He chose Pharaoh himself and all his wise men to school Moses in the experiences of leadership that would eventually lead to the deliverance of the people from the Egyptian Empire that had trained him.

The Season of preparation in Moses' life was two-fold. The second half was a season of humility in which he led a bunch of sheep around in the wilderness. There was no fancy life. There were no great accolades. There were no servants. There were sheep and there was time to think, time to hear from God, time to get all of the Egyptian junk separated from the leadership training and experience. Dr. Mike Murdock says, "Time is a weapon God has given us to search out the truth." Seasons of preparation take time.

King David's story demonstrates God's pattern again in 1st Samuel 15 - 2nd Samuel 2. David was a shepherd and the youngest of eight brothers. He was not considered much above the servants. But David had a destiny to be the warrior king of Israel. So, God began his training in the sheep pasture.

His warrior's heart was engaged when he saw lambs stolen by bears and lions; he attacked the predators and killed them. The Lord used the bravery David had learned on wild animals to move him to the next level of training.

In chapter 17 of 1st Samuel, David kills Goliath the giant and is taken to the castle of King Saul where he is trained in all matters of the court and all matters of war by the man he will replace. God often uses people who don't understand us, and whom we don't understand, to teach us. Sometimes it is because they are the ones we are going to replace. Even though we are going to replace them, we are not allowed to dishonor them by being lifted-up with pride. So here comes that difficult season of preparation that we just discussed in the lives of Joseph and Moses.

David is unjustly excommunicated by Saul and spends the next 10 years in various forms of hiding, learning the lesson of humility and learning to work with the warriors God sends him instead of the ones he wanted. During that season, he learns to put his pride aside over and over again. He learns to work with men of low degree; while Saul still has the great men of Israel in his army. He learns to face fools and not lose his temper; while wise men are trying to help Saul control his incontinent temper against David.

For Joseph and Moses and David that final season must have seemed like a complete waste, but God never wastes His appointed seasons of preparation. There are only a few ways in which a season of preparation can be wasted. First, and most obvious, we can refuse to go through it. Some choose this option for whatever reasons and leave very little evidence that destiny ever called. Others squander the season by refusing to learn. They go through the process and the pain but rebel against it until the lessons are lost and their negative attitude has left them un-promotable.

Seasons are windows of optimum preparation. If properly utilized, these "seasons" lay the foundation for expanding success in each subsequent season. If these same seasons are held in disregard as to their preparatory value, each will deficit the next and soon a negligent failure will have grown to debilitating proportions.

Three Imperative Preparations

So, let's ponder some practical processes of preparation. There are three separate things that must be prepared to lay proper foundations under any major enterprise we attempt, including the enterprise of life. We need to prepare the Person (ourselves) in Body, Soul and Spirit.

Chapter 6

Prepare the Person

The Body

In preparing the person, there are three areas of the person to focus on: body, soul and spirit. The most obvious is often over-looked: **the body**. People often dive right into ventures like business or marriage and do not consider what is needed physically to succeed. Properly assess the physical requirements of your future and prepare. It is simple, but it is very important. Often, people with wonderful aptitudes and attitudes for some particular thing disqualify themselves based on their physical conditioning and preparation. When our health crashes due to our own negligence, even if that negligence is cumulative over time, it is our own fault that we can't continue to do the things we enjoy and enjoy the things we do.

How broad is this disqualification epidemic? How many times does a single woman meet "Mr. Wonderful" but after a date or two it becomes obvious that she won't be able to participate in his recreational interests. She is deeply hurt when he decides to become "just friends" and the truth is he may be also, but if he is wise he will not continue to strengthen the connection with what will be a life of frustration. **Love may be willing to compromise but is it love if it demands compromise?**

We have three major areas to deal with to prepare the body: discipline, stamina and strength. The most important is discipline because it determines our success in the other two. Discipline is the premier issue of preparation because it determines what is in control, your will or your body.

Many consider the well-disciplined person to be obsessive, but the truth is, the disciplined have learned its value and enjoy a freedom that the undisciplined do not. They have the freedom to say "NO!" to their bodies and to temporary things. And they have the freedom to say yes to difficult things.

As I am writing this, hundreds of cyclists have pedaled past my house on some form of extended ride. (I know it is an extended ride because my house is ten miles from anywhere important and fifty miles from the nearest large city.) They were all disciplined people. There was a visible limit to how much overweight a person could be and still participate (maybe 50 lbs, and very few of them). Even though some stopped for a rest as if this trip were stretching their personal limits, they still pushed on toward their goal.

Those people are free to do this kind of thing that many others are not. Some were obviously novice riders, but others were just as obviously seasoned, conditioned riders with all the marks of discipline. Inquiry informed me that this trip started in a city 30 miles distant and has many to go after passing me. I am certain the first 10-20 miles determined who was disciplined and who was not.

The Apostle Paul said that bodily exercise profits a little bit compared to Godliness and many have used this excuse for their lethargy, incontinent appetite, license, and apathy. The greater statement by the Apostle on this topic is where he said, "I discipline my body and bring it into subjection . . ." (1st Corinthians 9:27). Paul was a man of exceptional stamina and we wonder at him but the key to his stamina is in that verse. Discipline is not about having a perfect body; it is about having a body that can and will do what you tell it to.

So then, we must practice telling our body "no" when it wants to "yes": no to more food, no to more sleep, no to another TV show, no to sex before marriage, no to the 6th can of Pepsi (Coke, Mt. Dew, whatever). We need to set some limits on ourselves. Draw a line in your mind (and on paper if you need to) that you will not cross.

We also must practice telling our body "yes" when it wants to "no." Tell it yes to do the dishes now rather than later, yes to vegetables, yes to writing that letter, yes to walking/jogging/running/cycling, yes to the alarm clock, yes to being on time for that appointment, yes to making a daily entry in the journal, yes to sex because you are married (the Bible's command not mine). Once again, we must have some personal minimums if we are ever going to reach our personal maximums.

As we continue with the ideas of stamina and strength, we would do well to redefine the "perfect" body. The perfect body is the body that can do what it enjoys and can enjoy what it does. That statement right there could salvage many vacations, careers, and marriages. For many, vacations are often just the same variety of inanity looking for a new place to happen, just finding a unique place to watch their favorite TV shows because their health cannot support any other activity. A second honeymoon shouldn't be the swan song of what was once engaging physical intimacy, but often it is, with only negligence to blame. It is a gross shame when someone who really enjoys their career or has a recognizable aptitude for it that makes it very satisfying, has to quit because they have allowed their health to disqualify them.

Stamina is one of the key elements of the "perfect" body. The benefits of building physical endurance are substantial. The increased blood flow to the brain benefits greatly our ability to focus and process information. Further, it helps regulate the endorphins that keep the brain and nervous system functioning. The blood flow also helps the body with healing itself and staying well. A body with great stamina can fight all forms of stress and disease better because it doesn't tire easily. A body with great stamina is prepared to take advantage of difficult opportunities and is prepared to survive disasters.

Remember,

****There is no such thing as luck! There is only the occasion where a specific level of preparedness meets with opportunity or disaster. *****

Furthermore, when the chips are down and everyone else is faltering under arduous endurance requirements, the person who lasts is the person who rises to the top or, in some cases, the only one who survives. The confidence, that you are capable of lasting through physical challenges, benefits every other area of attempted accomplishment. So, any preparation of the body should involve building stamina, staying power, reserves of energy.

Building stamina or endurance is challenging because it requires endurance. Each day that we pursue endurance we build endurance. That is why many people quit. And that is why discipline is the premier physical preparation. These preparations lean very heavily on each other. But they must be pursued. The process is simple (if someone talks like it is complicated, they are looking for excuses): (1) find a regimen you can do and then do it, consistently; (2) make sure that you perform progressively. A steady regimen that has inherent progression is the best way to acquire stamina because the progressive nature tends to keep us stretching and disciplined.

I have great respect for anyone that I see walking, jogging, or cycling as a regular regimen. They try! I place them and their behavior in another category. Some think that is unfair but thinking such is unwise. It is always our behavior that sets us apart from others. It should. It does. Behavior is a choice. We are responsible for it and are responsible to it. George Jones sang "Living and dying by the choices I've made." Preparing and maintaining our body is a choice we make.

Strength is a different kind of preparation. Though it will lean heavily on discipline and a little on stamina, strength is more mission specific. Your level of strength – what you can lift, or push, or pull, etc . . . – should be prepared according to your assignment particulars.

I have some friends who are Power Lifters. They need a level of strength that is rather ridiculous in comparison to the rest of us. They are called the Stand Strength Team and they perform evangelistic crusades with their feats of strength as the draw that gives them access to un-churched people. Two of their members have reached the level of bench pressing 600 lbs!

Most of us don't need that level of strength for our particular missions in life. But we do need some strength. Assessing our mission, then preparing for it is imperative. The only question that remains unanswered is one of your own personal initiative. Will you prepare?

Strength preparation will be more technical than stamina but still not prohibitively complicated. Research! Find someone who has succeeded at your particular assignment and inquire as to the physical challenges. Next find someone who knows how to build strength in that area of the body. Then do it!!

The tragedy is how many people are disqualified from something they want to pursue because they don't have the physical strength to handle the mission particulars. Less devastating, yet still unnecessary, is how many promotions in life are missed because people aren't strong enough to handle the particulars.

In the marching band, tuba players need a level of strength that is much higher than say, the flutists. Maybe it's nursing or paramedics that interests you and you think that you need all this knowledge to qualify and certainly you do, but I know a person who is presently disqualified from the field simply because she can't lift enough of a patient to continue.

Maybe you are totally white collar and figure you need only strength to lift a few file folders and a laptop but are your children part of your assignment? One of them may play football or con you into buying a horse or any number of other "blessings" that children lead us into. Will you be strong enough to fulfill that mission? When we prepare for our assignments we need to consider much more than just our commercial employment.

Chapter 7

Prepare the Person

The Soul

In preparing the person, the Soul is probably the most misunderstood because we don't define it accurately enough to know what we are working on. So, for this exercise we will define it as the seat and combination of the mind, will and emotions. The Mind is the planner and it needs, information. The will is the executor and it needs, opportunity. The Emotions are the expect-ers and the celebrators; they need HEEELLLLLLPP!!! Actually, the emotions need completion, or they live mostly in the realm of expectations and rarely get to celebrate; so en route to that completion, they need faith and hope. So then, how do we prepare these delicate and unquantifiable areas of our person?

Preparing the Mind

Prepare your mind by getting it information. In

Proverbs 2, Solomon speaks of four types of information: wisdom, discernment, understanding, and knowledge. For the sake of brevity, we must realize that nothing is accomplished without information. So, we need knowledge: general (parents, church, media and primary education) and specific (Secondary education and Mentors).

Time is a tool God has given us to gather information. In every season we must be gathering its information. Once we know what our specific information needs are, gathering with focus is our primary pursuit. While gathering general information becomes secondary it is still necessary because it helps us research our relevance.

Preparing the Will

The will is an interesting consideration. The sports coach, the military, and parents are generally the ones most concerned with preparing the will. Everyone else wants to know if the will is already prepared. Code words for this in the employment ads are "self-starter, self-motivated," and like statements. If the will is not trained to execute (launch, push, complete), there will be much talk but no action; most employers aren't interested in that.

The process of training the will is the simplest. Take action and follow through to completion. Now, underneath that simplicity is a far more technical process, but that process is worthless without this simplicity. The process begins with the mind. The mind must assess, plan, and project before the will can be effectively engaged. So, part of training the will is training the mind. But with the mind's part taken care of we can and should employ the will.

Actually, training the will can start in very small things. One of my favorite quotes is, "Leaders do what they know needs to be done without being told - with a good attitude." What does that mean? It means pick up your socks, hang up your clothes! It means there are some things that require very little assessment to determine the appropriate course of action. If you have to be told to do these things, your will is weak. Probably the training of the will starts with that statement.

Now comes the "in your face" stuff. Dr. Mike Murdock gives one of the best "will training" quotes ever. **"Never complain about anything!! Do something about it or shut up!!!"** It doesn't matter if its 20 lbs. clinging to your hips, a mouthy subordinate, a pushy boss, a 20-page English Literature paper; take action or be quiet!!! This is the essence of will preparation. The combination of mind and emotion too often lead to mouth instead of movement.

Train the will to take action by - taking action. First, in little things, then in progressively larger enterprises, until the soul (mind, will, and emotions) is a powerful, functioning force. Too much will, without the mind, will create a reactionary monster. Too much emotion will create a drama queen (or king, unfortunately). There is a powerful balance that makes for a properly functioning person, and that should be the main goal of our seasons of preparation. Therefore, we should move on to the one thing that upsets the balance most easily and deeply. Emotions!

Preparing the Emotions

If the physical body is the preparation that is often overlooked, then the emotions are the preparations that are run from! Because emotions are where we find our expectations, and because we want our expectations met, one of the best ways to prepare emotionally for the future is to forgive the past. We need to go through our past and deal with our unmet expectations.

We need to forgive in three areas. (1) We need to forgive human agents that appear to have failed us. (2) We need to forgive ourselves where it appears, or is blatantly obvious, that we have failed. (3) And we need to forgive God. Often, we hold God responsible because we believe that if a thing happened, He must have allowed it or planned it.

First of all, that is rather faulty reasoning. God uses earthly agents to accomplish much of His will and often those agents fail at their given assignments. Often, He sends us messages and messengers of warning to save us from disaster and we fail to heed them. But, even when we can find no earthly failure, and our inquiry goes unanswered, we need to forgive God for what we don't understand and trust His character which, according to His promises, the testimony of the saints, and the demonstrated ministry of Jesus, is good.

This topic of forgiveness can hardly be over-stressed. Forgiveness is the key that unlocks the shackles of bitterness. We often think that revenge will break those shackles but in reality, it only welds the shackles in place so that nothing can break them. Forgiveness changes the only person that matters, you! Revenge attempts to satisfy you and repay the offender, but neither are actually possible.

The scales of justice require mutuality as they should, but they can't very well restore losses of time, capital and opportunity. So, the end of the matter can only be reached through forgiveness. This is the truly peaceful place called closure, it exists nowhere else. That is why Jesus instructed us in the Lord's Prayer to forgive. He specifically stated that if we don't forgive, we can't be forgiven. Heaven will only be available to those who have already reached this peaceful rest.

As to the rest of the emotional preparedness process, there are simpler, though difficult, processes. First, we must learn how to adjust our expectations. Expectations are not wrong, but often our timetables for them are misguided. Because expectations are the link between the emotions and the mind. The secret to the expectations-game is two-fold: accurate information, and a willingness to make adjustments. Those two things are what allow emotions to make or break enterprises. From the slightest incidental relational encounters, to enterprises the size of Hitler's Third Reich. Prepare your emotions! Get them under the control of the Mind and Will, lest they destroy you!!

This is one of the tougher assignments. One of the subtle opportunities of the preparedness of a season. The process requires a very diligent observation of our own reactions. We have to train the mind and will to hold the emotions in check, until accurate information can be obtained, and processed. Then the process intensifies. The emotions have to be kept from clouding the conclusions of the mind, and from dictating improper objectives to the will.

Every season brings with it certain emotional encounters. We need to learn early to control those emotions. That doesn't mean that we stifle them as the Stoics of ancient times; that means we train ourselves as to when and how we release them. There are situations that we encounter where our emotions will be deeply engaged but will also jeopardize our objective. Being in control of those emotions will make or break us, will determine success or failure, will be the determining factor in our survival.

Emotions are one of the quickest things to lead us out of season. Mr. or Miss Wonderful comes along out of season and shows interest, maybe makes offers and commitments. If the emotions cloud the mind and will, here, we are going out of season. Think of the young parents as they experience the birth of their child. The rush of emotion is such as never encountered before, and it should be. However, some young parents lose sight of objectives under the weight of these new emotions, and can't bring themselves to engage the necessary discipline to raise the child correctly. Now a season is being wasted because untrained emotions are given control over the mind and the will. Many jobs are lost to uncontrolled emotions which are really untrained emotions. We need to exit every season having learned how to better control our emotions.

Chapter 8

Prepare the Person

The Spirit

There is yet one rock of personal preparedness that can destroy us or employ us. It is the spirit. Once again, let's define what we are talking about. **The Spirit of a man is the seat of his divinity, the shelter of his conscience and the catalyst of his character.** Now before I get shot by all of my preacher friends for being a humanist, let me clarify what I mean by "seat of divinity". Man is a spirit being. Man is created in the image of God. That doesn't make him God but does mean that God put an undeniable connection between Himself and us. This is the divinity that I am speaking of - this eternal requirement within us - creates a curiosity and capacity, for the supernatural; but there is a problem.

We are born spiritually dead! The apostle Paul calls us "You who were dead in trespasses and sins . . ." This is the result of sin, specifically original sin. The term "original sin," is a theological term that simply means this: Adam and Eve, as the original humans, were created without sin; but afterward sinned, and thereby plunged the whole of mankind (their offspring) into the darkness of spiritual deadness. What had been a face-to-face relationship with God was diminished to a relationship accessed only by faith and a system of sacrifice.

God was far more unhappy with this, than mankind had the capacity to imagine. So, He launched the "Plan of Salvation" that had been in reserve since the first consideration of giving man a free will. (God's love for us would not allow Him to give us a free-will without making provision for our redemption should we actually choose to sin.) Jesus came, entering this world through Mary's virgin womb, lived a sinless life, preached the good news of salvation for three years, then in the ultimate act of love for us and obedience to God's plan, paid the price for that salvation with His own death, and delivered us from spiritual death through His own resurrection from the dead.

We still access salvation by faith, but it is now faith in the Son of God, Jesus the Christ, and it is real relationship, complete with authority, power and inheritance.

The Apostle Paul gives us great news and assurance when He informs us that we "have been made alive..." through the "Spirit of Him who raised Christ from the dead." This is the premier preparation of the spirit man. We need to be made alive. **We need to be brought out of the death-bondage of sin, into the abundant-life freedom in Christ Jesus.** Jesus, himself, speaking of this change said, "You must be born again." Indeed, our dead spirit must be born of the Spirit of God to make us wholly alive as He intended.

The process is simple: Confess and repent of your sins; Believe on the Lord Christ Jesus (that His sacrifice is sufficient for your forgiveness); and You Will be saved. This is as simple as praying, "Lord I know I am a sinner. I am very sorry about that. Please forgive my sins. I believe in Your Son Christ Jesus and that His sacrifice paid the penalty for my sins. Thank you for saving me, in Jesus Name." Jesus and the Father say back to you, "Neither do I condemn you. Go and sin no more." It really is that simple. This exchange of faith between you and God awakens your spirit man, and the process of you following God and reaching His dreams for you, will have begun. Whatever season of life you are in, this preparation needs to be completed with great haste.

The Conscience

This presentation of the spirit man began with three areas; we have covered one. The second thing in our list is that the spirit of a man is the shelter of his conscience. Very simply, the conscience is the one thing in the spirit of a man that is active even before he is born of the Spirit. **The conscience is the "God installed" barometer of the soul, that is located in our spirit man.** It warns us of behaviors and thought processes that are out of order.

The conscience, taken out of the shelter of the spirit, can be perverted by bad information. Secular humanism has done this in the education systems to the point that young people can no longer get good information from their consciences. This was never more evident than in the Columbine High School Massacre.

Here were two young men from apparently stable middle-class homes who turned on their classmates and teachers in a conscienceless spree of premeditated violence. Their homes are not where they received that ridiculous information, it was the education system that taught them to hate Christians and athletes and taught them that God's Laws are not <u>real</u> boundaries. The foolishness of Darwinian Humanism falsely taught them the theory of "survival of the fittest," which led them to believe that "might is right"; and if the "might," can't be accepted by others, then suicide is the way to exit from the *consequences of* that might.

The early seasons of life are the most favorable to developing and forming the conscience, into the accurate tool of the spirit, that it needs to be. That being said, there is no excuse for not having a properly formed and informed conscience. The season you are in now is the best season for informing that conscience. Begin by reading God's information. The Ten Commandments in Exodus 20; the Great commandments stated by Jesus in Matthew 22:37-40; the commands to love one another in John 13:34; 15:12,13,17, and finally Paul's description of love in 1st Corinthians 13. There are many other things in the scripture to inform our conscience such as Proverbs, the Epistle of James, and the writings of the Prophets. Do it now and begin to reduce the odds of a misinformed conscience, leading you toward a maladjusted Character.

The Character

Now, character is the practical goal of spiritual preparation; and as its catalyst, the spirit, motivates that character development. Here we establish "Who we are." There is not enough space in this discussion of our "Seasons of Optimum Preparation," to deal with this topic in any thoroughness. A book with a specific focus on this topic will be forthcoming and will be presented in the context of Protocol: being the right person in your time and place.

For the space we have here it will have to suffice to say that the preparation of character will be the determining factor in our long-term survival and success of any enterprise including the enterprise of life. Prepare your character well. How?

Determine your minimums: the behavioral lines you will not fall below in each area of life. **Determine your disciplines:** the level at which you will function, the amount of yourself you will pour into each enterprise and relationship. **Determine your relational boundaries:** who you will and will not make covenants with. **Determine your core values:** what you believe - and practice them as virtues (What you really believe determines your actions, as opposed to what you say you believe.) Let this scripture be your guide:

(Galatians 5:22-23) "But the fruit of the Spirit is love, joy, peace, longsuffering, kindness, goodness, faithfulness, [23] gentleness, self-control. Against such there is no law."

Segment 3

Season of Preparation

The Structures

When we have prepared our personhood to be a strong foundation capable of supporting our dreams and assignments, we must then prepare a structure that will protect and perpetuate them. Too often, people work very hard to become a person of consequence in their chosen endeavors; then they surround themselves with an obstructive environment that will frustrate and defeat them. Let's now consider the next tier of preparations:

Prepare the Environment

Prepare the Relationships

Chapter 9

What is Relevant?

Environment is so often a tricky thing. I am writing from my home in rural Michigan. It is an area with many small towns and villages that were flourishing a century ago. At the time, the industries were lumber and farming. The area was only settled by 50 years, the farms were fresh, the lumber was just finishing its run and still quite relevant. The rail lines ran in a grid that went north and south and east and west every 40 miles.

Now, the rails are gone. There are only 4 trunk lines going North, one from Detroit, one from Lansing, one from Grand Rapids and the last up the west coast from Muskegon. There are none that go east to west north of the line between Detroit and Grand Rapids. The environment changed.

No one is coming into Michigan to build new Railroads because there is no idea on how they would profit. Our farms are old and vanishing, lumber has become quite local in the sense that raw logs rarely travel more than 80 miles to get to a mill unless they are specialties like veneer which has become rare in this state. There was an Oil and Gas boom for about 30 years (1935- 1965?) but it didn't produce the kind of traffic to support the railroads.

I really think that the line that formerly ran through my town would have made a great scenic railroad as it passed through the farmland on its way to the beautiful Grand Traverse bay area, but the railroad companies and controllers lost the vision for passenger-rail in the 1950's when everyone bought a car. Such a rail would have needed to survive 20 years (the same 20 years that saw trucking replace the trains in the freight business) to get to the first real rise in oil prices that would have caused people to consider commuting by train and 50 years before the price jumped enough to make it feasible. When the big gas-price jump came in 2004-5, the rail had been torn up for 15 years. The need was there but the preparations for it were prohibitive. There was no longer a structure to improve and launch from other than the railroad grade: no steel rails, no wooden ties, aging and unmaintained trestles, stations long since bought by private parties for offices and other use or fallen into gross disrepair. Now it's just a raised grade with a walk-trail. The environment cannot be improved economically, need or no need.

Before we leave the "relevance" line of thought, let's shift our minds to a more local and even personal perspective. **Environment cannot be separated from relationships.** Have you ever known someone (or maybe you are that someone) who has a dreadful bent toward "fatal attractions"? They have plenty of aptitude, plenty of training, they're hard-working, and very productive when on task, and yet still unsuccessful. Then one day we meet part of their inner circle

- best friend, wife, mother/father, etc… - and we realize they are linked to someone completely juxtaposed to their assignment. They have perpetual sources of negativity, disbelief, and opposition that drain away their productivity and focus.

We don't need to look far. In the modern era there have been several professional athletes whose stories are very stark in contrast to others. The great success stories like Cal Ripken Jr., Nolan Ryan, Deon Sanders, John Elway, Charles Barkley, Carl Malone, etc . . . have all been great motivational stories with so many high points, but there are contrasts.

I'm thinking of an athlete who attached himself to a gossip-magazine socialite with obvious conduct and relational issues. Twice the poor athlete has nearly killed himself in trying to drown out the internal sorrow this woman has brought on him. I'm thinking of some others who never separated from their "thug friends in the hood" and before long, those people were taking them back into the drugs and violence lifestyles that professional sports had helped them escape. Soon, they were in prison for some altercation or some drug charge for which there was no sensible explanation.

As I typed this paragraph I stopped halfway through to do a search of crimes committed by professional athletes and was shocked. The number of crimes that were directly attributable to the people with whom the athletes surrounded themselves was predominant. Amazing!

Whatever our assignment is, there will be an optimum environment for it and there will be disastrous environments (often having more to do with relationships than with street corners) that will not in any way support it. This is inescapable. Preparing that environment and our expectations of it is prerequisite to accomplishment.

Chapter 10

What does the Bible Demonstrate?

The Apostle Paul called himself "the Apostle to the Gentiles". Without question, that was what he accomplished with his life and so the title goes unchallenged. But who Paul was in that environment and how that environment was right and ripe for him, is the point of our consideration.

The eleven disciples who started the church in the book of Acts were Jews and mostly from Galilee. They were men of no broad reputation and of no status in the Roman Empire. The Romans were already annoyed with the dispersed Jews and were on short temper with the Jews of Jerusalem. When Christianity birthed and began to grow, it was considered another sect of Judaism. Such a consideration brought down much persecution on the people of "The Way" as they were called. These disciples were at risk in Jerusalem; disposing of them in the regions of the Roman empire beyond Jerusalem would have been done in a hurry and without thought by Roman authorities.

Paul comes into the picture and turns it all upside down. He is a natural born citizen of the Roman City of Tarsus. This was to make all the difference in his ability to evangelize all over the Roman Empire. On more than one occasion this status freed him from incarceration and on other occasions saved him from execution at the hands of both Romans and Jews. After being beaten in the Macedonian city of Philippi, his declaration of Roman Citizenship brought such fear to the city officials that they came to the jail in person to release him and beg that he leave quietly. In Jerusalem, the Jewish religious leaders were determined to kill him, but his citizenship again saved him and gave him audience before the governor. It seems that God prepared him for his mission to the Roman empire at large.

This wasn't the only way in which he was key to the environment around him. One of the great challenges to early Christianity was a major push by its Jewish converts to bring the Gentiles under Mosaic Law. Paul was just the man to deal with this heresy. He was a Pharisee, highly educated to what would be comparably doctoral status in our day. The eleven disciples were quite uneducated in all the commentative nuances that made up the Judaism of the day. However, Paul (as Saul of Tarsus) was a Pharisee trained under Gamaliel, one of the most respected Rabbis of the day and in a school that was multi-generational. He was no middling scholar and was quite impervious to attacks by the dispersed Jews. Most of his Epistle to the Galatians deals with this very issue. He was prepared in every way for the environment to which his assignment took him.

Yet, there is one more way in which Paul prepared his environment. He was quite particular in His companions. It should be said that his first evangelistic partner was chosen by God (details in Acts 13) but it should also be noted that this man, Barnabas, had proven himself as someone who believed in Paul's value to the Church. Barnabas was the one who went looking for Paul when he had returned to Tarsus. Barnabas and Saul delivered offerings of benevolence to the saints in Jerusalem during a drought. This was a "Qualified Relationship" as far as Paul was concerned.

Paul and Barnabas had great success on their first Evangelistic tour, when a young protégé, John Mark, had started with them but failed to finish the tour. Paul considered this weakness and would not take the young man with them a second time. Barnabas wanted to cultivate the faith and discipline of John Mark, somewhat in the way he had searched for and helped Paul (though the comparison wasn't equitable). Paul was so exclusive about who could be near this arduous, fast paced and often dangerous assignment that he and Barnabas parted ways and Paul chose Silas. Silas turned out to be a companion who could sing in a dungeon after a beating!! Quite worthy he was, of this partnership with Paul.

Let's ask the pertinent question for us. Have we qualified the relationships with us by the considerations of the environment of our assignments? We must understand that relationships make up our emotional environment and whether or not they support us in the great challenges of our assignments may make or break us. Are we dragging a troop of clingers from a past that we are desperately trying to escape? Who is in your life right now that is constantly putting down your pursuit of your dream?

Let's ask this the other way: who is in your life that is fighting your vices and is constantly turning your face toward your successful future? It's time to make some choices. One group seems to be fun at the moment but are really only using you to surfeit their immediate whimsy for meaningless events and distractions. The other sees great potential in you and is fighting to get that real, undistracted, uninhibited "you" some room to run for your assignment.

Chapter 11

Preparing the Environment

Seasons of preparation look to the future. We need to assess what the environment of our future will be. Let me offer more detailed instructions. To assess the environment, we are traveling into, we need to be examining variables and constants. The variables we are looking for are these: controlled variables and uncontrolled variables. The constants are fixed entities, both natural and spiritual.

What are the controllable variables? These are the things that you can directly affect the function of. Therefore, Controlled Variables need to be controlled! You are the primary controlled variable. You are the one thing that you can control, so control yourself. We control the number of hours we will work, the amount of energy we will invest in our destiny. Now that is you, but are there controlled variables external to you?

Well, like the circles of a stone splash in a pond, you have some control over the things closest to you. You control who your friends are. You have some control over who you associate with and who you allow to be near you. This paragraph will reappear in my book on Boundaries, so I can abbreviate such a discussion here. It simply needs to be said that in preparing your environment, work for control of who is allowed to be around you, your dreams, your work.

Things like tools, training and information, are controlled variables. Furthermore, there are things that we can work toward control of, such as, credit and cash flow. These are things over which you have direct control in the season of preparedness.

Uncontrolled variables require a different kind of preparation. **Uncontrolled variables must be compensated for.** We must learn to consider potential contingencies and then pre-plan our adjustments to them. The great Peter Daniels[3] says, "Plan your problems." Relationships are one of the easiest ways to demonstrate uncontrolled variables. We are often misunderstood. People react in ways contrary to our expectations. But communication should not be an "all or nothing" gamble because relationships are far too important to every aspect and enterprise of life. We have very little control over how the other person reacts, so we need to build and maintain a resilient attitude, an attitude that forgives and seeks solutions to communication problems.

Things like the weather are uncontrolled variables. We actually prepare our evasive actions ahead of time. I ride motorcycles in Northern Michigan, so I carry a jacket, rain gear, and leather chaps in my saddle bags.

Competitors and competition are mostly uncontrolled variables. We need to project what the competitions will be in the environment that we are heading into, then prepare our expectation for compensations and prepare our compensations.

Constants are the things that do not change. The four weather seasons are static. While they may vary in intensity they are still what they are every year. In many places, the roads are fixed entities. The Highway is where it is and wishing won't move it. The geographical features of an area are mostly fixed entities.

Constants must be capitalized on. They must be turned to our favor. Pikes Peak, in Colorado Springs, Co, is the fixed feature of that area. Zebulon Pike (for whom it is named) saw it as an unconquerable obstruction that would never be climbed, but within 60 years of his doubtful declaration, there was a fancy hotel at the bottom, a cog railway to the top and a restaurant on the top. The city of Colorado Springs now has 4-5 reservoirs built on the sides of the mountain to catch the rain and snow-melt and supply fresh water to the region. Look around you. There are so many examples of people turning the constants of their environment to their advantage that it is not necessary to continue giving examples here.

We need to prepare for the constants of our environment by preparing ourselves with adjusted expectations, proper tools, and plans for contingencies and leveraging.

Chapter 12

Prepare the Relationships

The last of the three great preparations is one of the most difficult: **Preparing the Relationships**. The whole of this preparation is contained in a couple of very plain commands in the Scripture. In the Old Testament, the prophet proclaimed the command of the Lord to be, "Let every man speak truth to his neighbor". And in the New Testament Jesus reiterated this command when he taught, "Let your 'yes' be yes and your 'no' be no. Everything else is of the devil!!"

Preparing relationships is all about **communication.** So, in your season of preparation for things like marriage, business, charitable service, etc... communicate your expectations and commitments clearly and effectively. Tell the truth about environment, variables, constants, tools and training. This is the essence of Preparing Relationships. Many engagements, and lesser levels of romantic relationships, have ended when someone ran into a situation about which they were not informed - such as the rest of the family. (Uncle Ralph or Aunt Hilda may be eccentric but if one is warned one can prevent being drawn into some awful ordeal like skunk trapping; taking the pet howler monkey for a walk in the mall; helping deliver the home-remedy elixir to various customers under the cover of darkness.) (It is also nice to know who to stand upwind of at a particular function.) Communicating properly does not guarantee response but it does at least give the other person the opportunity to inform you of what encounters will cause them to commit a felony on your person.

If communication and information are available and accurate we can prepare relationships in a couple of other ways. Once again, my intention is to write extensively on this topic of relationships in the book on boundaries; however, I wish to mention it here briefly for the purpose of making use of our seasons of preparation. The second way to prepare relationships is to qualify them. We need to qualify the people who we allow to be near us. The season of preparation is the time to do this, before we launch into the season of covenant with a person. There must be some minimums that we expect of people before we deepen the relationships.

We also must qualify ourselves for relationships with the people that we deem necessary, desirable, productive, epic, as destiny. A great question to ask yourself is, "Have I found someone I desire to give to; or only someone I want to take from?" Often, we wish and even hope for a relationship in the selfish wallow of unpreparedness. It is a gross travesty on the word love and an insult to the idea of real desire, for us to think that the person we love and desire, that drew us to themselves by some virtue that was new to us, in the end should tarnish and stain - even give up - that virtue to accommodate us.

The statement, "I just want to be accepted for who I am." Ought to mean, "I want to be accepted for my gifts

and talents, my aptitudes, my assignment from God, for the me I was created to be." But usually it means, "I want to be accepted for the me I've become with all my vices, weaknesses, negligence, for the me I refuse to change, the me I've destroyed."

If the previous paragraph shocked you some, then you are probably one of those who believe you have a right to your fits, your fat, your failure. **I don't apologize! On the contrary I choose to vehemently fight for the person God created you to be that is suffocating somewhere underneath that façade!** Your season of preparedness should be employed in the process of breaking that clay mask off your life; and qualifying for the real you to start experiencing the joy of living what God planned for you!

The end goal of qualifying relationships is for you to be prepared to commit to those relationships. As you leave the season of preparedness, you should have gathered the necessary information about relationships, to allow you to determine with whom you are going to share your life – time, genius and capital – your dreams, your fears, your celebrations, your mourning, your accomplishments and your failures. You need to commit to someone who really is competent and safe to share those things with. If you finish your season of preparedness with quality, qualified commitments to quality, qualified individuals, you will be **ready** to move on to the next season, and specifically a season in which you harvest the good of your preparations. Committing over top of unpreparedness will also give you a harvest, but it will be the consequences of your negligence.

Segment 4

Season of Investment

Thus, says the LORD, your Redeemer, The Holy One of Israel: "I am the LORD your God, Who teaches you to profit, Who leads you by the way you should go. (Isaiah 48:17)

Seasons are windows of optimum investment. The idea of investment has to do with Resources and properly targeting those resources.

.

Chapter 13

What is Relevant?

Let me go back to the college example. That is the optimum time to invest in academic learning. When we get to our chosen field, we become too busy to spend much time on academics. A medical student can pour himself into his studies while in school but give him a wife, two kids, a practice, 6 patients per hour, his rounds at two local hospitals, and academics become a far-flung memory.

Consider construction projects. When the building is being built, investments are easy to implement. While the building is only rafters and a roof, any decision about climate control systems can easily and efficiently be put into action. However, once we have built the building and leased the space out, deciding to change the climate control system becomes gravely more expensive. There are now customers coming and going from the various businesses. There are now a hundred employees in the way. There are now finished walls that will have to be altered to make changes and, in some cases, torn out to have access to the original climate control system. There was an optimum season for that investment.

Investing out of season may be necessary from time to time, but it always involves more expense, more discomfort, more trauma, more stress, and this will be true financially, emotionally, and relationally.

Consider financial investments toward retirement. There is an optimum time for that investing that will start with very small sums deposited consistently which in turn build with compounding interest into a very large account. As the years go by the clock for the value of compound interest will tick down and the only way to achieve retirement stability of income will be to deposit a very large lump sum.

So, it is with business investing. Many people have wonderful ideas that can be developed into very rewarding profitability, but they want all the profit up front instead of realizing that some capital should be turned back into the business for better equipment, for training, for contingencies. Many businesses fail because a little bit of greed in the beginning destroys the expanded profitability of the future.

It is the same in relationships. When I do premarital counseling, I recommend to most couples to wait one to three years before they begin having children. It is a wonderful season to invest in the marriage relationship. All too often this season is circumvented by the arrival of a baby and the emotional economy switches from lovers to parenting. It is very easy for the work of relational investing to be redirected completely into the children, creating a distance and eventually a vacuum that destroys the very reason the family came into being. There is an optimum time for investing in the marriage itself and that is before the children arrive.

Assessing our season for what needs to be invested, allows us to focus our resources well. Once again, this will create an environment of confidence and peace that will bring joy to living.

Chapter 14

What do the Scriptures show us?

Let's consider the Biblical examples of this relationship between "what time it is" and our investments. The scripture says, "Train a child in the way he should go and when he is old he will not depart from it." (Proverbs 22:6) This proverb has everything to do with seasons of investment. A child should not be trained primarily on the basis of how it helps them at the moment. A child should be trained with a vision of what they will need to be competent as an adult. The return on the investment is rather distant though it may be set in the context of their immediate situation.

The first thing the wise man tells us is to **train**. That does not mean that we necessarily profit immediately. Training is always investing. It is always major investment with minor return. Being greedy can have more to do with our maturity than our money. Too many people are so "greedy" for an immediate return on anything they do that they never do anything. There is a mindset that says, "If I can't have everything up-front, I won't participate." People of this mindset don't bother with investing.

The second thing we note in the sage's recommendation is that we **train** a **child**. There is no season better for establishing the productive and healthy habits and rhythms of life than in the early developmental stages of a child's life. Their hygiene, their manners, their social skills, their response to authority, their focus, their perseverance, are best developed before they are 12 years old.

Now, the next word is crucial: the **"Way"** the child should go speaks of setting the direction of the child by investing in the child's living skills. They must be trained to consider, to plan, to engage, to persevere, and to finish. They must be trained in protocol so that they know how to act in specific situations. They need training in timing, when to speak or refrain, when to hurry or wait, when to fight or escape. They need training in boundaries so that they know where they should and should not be, who they should and should not be with, and how to discover such at the lowest "life cost."

I am quite certain that some who read this will say, "I never received that training. Is it too late? Have I missed my season? Can I recover from this deficit?" I mentioned earlier in this chapter that **investing out of season may be necessary, but it will be more expensive and more difficult.** Adjust your expectations to the task necessary and get to work. There is no benefit in continuing to circumvent the necessary. Every day we wait to start investing is an expanded and even exponential loss when harvest begins. Figure out what you are missing and start investing toward it immediately. Changing and establishing new "ways" is always possible, though time will make it less probable. So . . .

The worst time to start investing, the wrong day for investing, is tomorrow. _Tomorrow is one of the most fragile_

ideas ever considered in the universe!! It only exists in the realm of planning. It is forever in the womb of hope; for when it is born it will be renamed "today" and will declare to the world our investment in it.

If it is so imperative that we start investing today, "what, where and how" questions leap to the mind. I don't know that this instructional venture is capable of dealing with the investment specifics of how and where because each consideration is situationally specific, so let's look at some principle areas that will point us to our particulars.

The idea of investment has to do with Resources and properly targeting those resources. I would like to consider three resources as paramount to this writing's objective: Time, Genius and Capital.

Chapter 15

Resource 1

Time

Time is the most precious of commodities because it is the hardest to replenish. While the scripture does say that wisdom will lengthen our days and also says that the Lord will restore the years the locusts have eaten, we must also consider Paul's admonition to "redeem the time because the days are evil". The moment you have just lived, has been lived. Dr. Ed Cole, speaking of reputation, says what took years to build can be torn down and destroyed in one moment's rash act.

Time needs to be employed with the utmost accuracy because each moment properly invested now impregnates the future's moments with expanded returns. Each moment foolishly invested now impregnates the future's moments with diminished returns. Particularly in the realm of time we must consider desired returns.

I spent a great portion of this book on Seasons of preparation and it would be easy to ride that "hobby horse" here, therefore I would like to shift focus within the topic of

Time to look at how we spend our time when we have moved out beyond the main season of preparation.

Peter Daniels[3] observed in the lives of great men and woman one crucial element: they had a sense of destiny. They knew "what time it was," or more specifically, they knew when it was "their time". This is crucial in every one of the topics we have touched in this book. We need to know when we have passed from preparation to performance. It has definitive impact on how we spend our time.

There comes a point in romantic relationships where a well-run courtship of investigation, comradery, bonding and unifying has run its course and it is time to commit. The preparatory season is over, and it is time to invest our time in the next season.

So, it is in careers and business. There is a time for gathering information, acquiring skills, making plans, making projections and there is a time for committing to a process of implementation, for launch, for management, for completion. We need to know this time and then invest our time in the employments of our destiny. There comes a time when the professor is not there, the drill instructor is with his next class, your mentor is in his office writing a book, and you are alone in the field. It is time to put what you know to the test. If you fail here, all of your tools will become rusty, some outdated. Your skills will atrophy, and your training will lose its relevance.

Failure at this juncture produces interesting interviews. People give thousands of reasons for failure that can often be reduced to the simple misuse of minutes. When we hear some

Blues or Country music artist howling about wasted days and even years, we shouldn't start singing with them; we should start contemplating how such a thing happens. Most often it happens through minor distractions. A thirty-minute TV program leads into a second program and then a third and before we know it, the project out in the garage that was promised to an acquaintance who is willing to pay us, has fallen behind. That person has a friend with a similar project that is hoping they have found a person who can complete it with excellence, but now the delays make them look elsewhere.

This is actually how failure happens - not big catastrophes, just little choices that aren't really wrong but are detrimental to progress and accomplishment. I mentioned TV but what if I mentioned Facebook, or video games, or internet surfing (some of which is harmless and then some that is not so harmless). Let me be honest - this book has taken waaaayyyy toooo loong to complete. (I shall now do some introspective assessment.)

It is imperative that we know how to invest our time productively.

Chapter 16

Resource 2

Genius

First, let's define what we are *not* talking about. We are not talking about the classmate who could do all the algebra and geometry in his head. We are not talking about that same classmate, now a snob walking around in his adult life waving his degrees at everyone. We are not talking about the hermit down at the end of the dead-end road with 32 half-finished inventions in his barn and 20 more strewn about his yard.

At the same time, we are not talking about that one friend we all have who stands looking at a situation of challenge and then says, "I've got an idea. Hold my drink and watch this!" If you stand too close to that guy, serious injury could happen to you and the snob and the hermit from down the dead-end road.

"That's nothing! Hold my drink and watch this!!!!" is not genius!!

I probably should take the edge off of my insinuations here by saying that these people may actually have some of this thing called genius in them, but too often those of us who don't walk around in such perpetual states of oddity are inclined to believe that those people are the geniuses and we are just not in that classification of people. And that is our mistake.

Genius is a unique resource in that it has very little accurate measure. Men have tried for years to measure it with things like the IQ tests but mostly only accomplished a "pigeon-holing" of people that those people defy daily when they pursue the things they are passionate about. **Genius is that "creative aptitude" for some particular activity or calling.** Genius is unique in that it can be improved and expanded through knowledge and practice. You have heard it said, "She has a 'way' with children," or "he has a 'way' with words." We describe people as having a sense for something beyond technical training. Sometimes in music we say, "that person has a real 'feel' for the music," or the rhythm or for a particular instrument. It may not be proper to label these people geniuses but rather to say that they have genius in them as we all do for some particular thing.

Genius cannot be seen and therefore requires faith to be engaged. Often people trapped in negative thought patterns and depression have lost faith and therefore their genius has dried up. They don't see themselves able to change themselves or their circumstances and so they quit thinking. They begin to live vicariously through the lives of others via TV, children, gossip, or they turn incorrigibly negative and spread their hopelessness to everyone else. Often these people blame others for everything allowing bitterness to nail the coffin shut on their genius.

The invisibility of genius causes many people to pass over it in considering the equation of success in their lives. They often consider time because it seems to be running out and they consider capital because they don't have enough to meet obligations or access the tools and lifestyle they prefer. But Genius can often solve both issues, it just requires the most faith to employ. The biblical reference to genius would be wisdom. Proverbs tells us to acquire wisdom as paramount to other resources because it helps us use both time and capital wisely.

It is Genius that helps us when we are out of sync with our seasons. It is that creative aptitude that helps us when we are behind, to find ways to compensate. The old fashion Green-house is a great example of this. With the proliferation of glass windows, some wise guy in a cold climate realized that the sun warmed through windows wonderfully and he began to wonder if he could set frost sensitive plants in planters in that "window protected" sunlight and expand his growing season. Presto! Creative genius overcame seasonal challenges. Genius helped him manipulate time in favor of capital. Amazing! But simple!

Genius is almost always the creative application to produce previously unknown cooperation between things and entities that already exist. Men boiled water in pots for years. They watched the steam rise faster and in more volume as the water increased in temperature. One day a fellow thought, "I wonder if that steam were pushed through a whistle would it make the same sound as when I blow through the whistle?" Then he put a whistle device on his teapot and we had the whistling teapot. But later, another fellow saw the steam coming through the small ports of the teapot whistle and wondered how much force could be produced by capturing the steam in a closed system like a piston. Presto! The steam engine is born. All of the necessary elements for these things were already there - the water, the pot, the whistle, the steel to make a piston system - but these men creatively combined things into cooperative systems and changed first, the cottage kitchen, and later, the world. That is Genius

This kind of Genius can also be found in administrative management, in leadership communication, in business-to-business networking, in marketing and many other endeavors. Everyone has some genius in them for something. In most people, it lies undiscovered, crusted over and captivated by negative thinking and poor information sources.

Genius is the most powerful of our resources because it can compensate for the deficiencies in both time and capital. We should work very hard to expand our genius in the things about which we are passionate. It can make all the difference when the "chips are down".

Chapter 17

Resource 3

Capital

Capital is the most visible and therefore the easiest to trust-in and the easiest by which to be deceived. The Scripture constantly warns us of the deceitfulness of riches, of how riches are fleeting, of how they require excessive managing, stringent boundaries and exemplary moral fortitude to handle properly. Capital is a very converse resource because it diminishes rapidly with hoarding and provides no comfort to soul or body; but it is increased through proper investing and produces wonderful things when it is expended properly. Capital is never about the having; it is always about the investing.

Considering that the Bible is so vocal on the dangers of capital, it is of interest what it says about it in a constructive way. In more than one place, the scripture calls capital seed. Seed is different than grain. Grain is for consumption after the harvest, but seed is set aside for planting. Grain is stored to preserve flavor; seed is stored to preserve germination.

What does this really have to do with anything? And will the author explain the parable please? This exercise is about proper use of seasons and that makes all the difference with capital. We must know (learn and practice) when it is time to plant and when it is time to harvest. Is it time to consume, to enjoy the benefits of it, or is it time to bury in faith, and experience the temporary loss of it?

The real question then is, do we own the capital or does the capital own us? A cliché? Yes. Accurate? Also, yes. We think we "own" through possession, but **the reality is we only "own" if we are "free to employ the capital,"** as opposed to "free to access it". Money is not your servant until you can invest it. Until then, even though we may have enough to acquire trinkets, toys and tools, we are in a stalemate, at best, and potentially a disadvantage, hinting at bondage to the very money we crave.

One of the scriptures that describes capital in terms of seed says a most interesting thing. "Now may He who supplies seed to the sower, and bread for food, supply and multiply the seed you have sown and increase the fruits of your righteousness. . ." This verse is full of information for us. First, we see that it is God who gives seed - and it says He gives. The obvious question becomes, who does he give too? He gives to sowers and to consumers but there are ample scriptures to demonstrate Gods' preference for sowers. Why? First, the planters become partners with Him. God is always seeking relationship with us and when we show the wisdom of working His systems of prosperity, He becomes eager to complete that partnership.

Second, sowing or planting takes faith; faith connects with and pleases God. Faith is the interactive principle that connects us with the supernatural. In Hebrews chapter 11, we are told that it is impossible to please Him without faith. **IMPOSSIBLE!!** That is more than just a hint about how valuable God considers faith. So, when we demonstrate the mastery of the capital He has helped us access by being able to plant/invest it in faith, He becomes very pleased with us. It is an escalating process of partnership and relationship.

It also says He gives bread for food. That is the other end of the sowers' task – to harvest. Further, to the sower there is the context of the whole verse which is Paul's Prophetic proclamation that God will multiply seed and harvest. It should be undeniable; understanding from these verses that God is looking for partners in His original intent, which was to give man dominion to manage the creation and experience increase in that management. This is the real way to properly use capital in the season of investment. In the process of partnership and relationship with God.

Segment 5

Windows of Optimum Productivity

The Season of Efficiency

"So, I sent messengers to them, saying, 'I am doing a great work, so that I cannot come down. Why should the work cease while I leave it and go down to you?'" (Nehemiah 6:3)

Is the time right for the most efficient use of our energies and activities? Optimum productivity has to do with the efficiency of the season. Efficiency is very connected to focus. To determine if we are making the most efficient use of our season, we really evaluate our focus. The more accurately we assess our season, the more efficiently we can apply our energy and activity.

Chapter 18

What is Relevant?

So then, let us consider this, here in the modern day. Much too often people are busy expending energy on activities, but the activities have very little to do with their goals and dreams. Though an activity may have purpose integral to itself, that purpose may not be connected to anything that is really important to the individual performing it. Rick Warren's "Purpose Driven Life" is recommended reading on this topic. Probably the starkest picture of this is when someone is asked to participate in a mid-week or special service at church and their excuse is their favorite TV show. Is the TV show funny? Dramatic? Informative? Maybe it is all of the above, but does it have any comparison at all to the great work of the Gospel.

Let me touch the great secular sacrament of our time – school sports. Sports have intrinsic values, some of which have already been presented in the chapter on preparing the person. I do not deny that those benefits are there. However, we need to look at a much larger picture. People, supposedly committed to the church, and the great ideal of their children going to heaven and amounting to something for God on the way, will skip church with the kid and throw mama and the preacher from the train to accommodate that kid and the ball team.

So, let's stretch the example another level without departing from truth, at all, but rather by touching it in its raw form without glossing over its scarred underside. It is often in this school sports setting that a good Christian kid is exposed to the idea that people who go to church are weak and uncommitted to real things like winning and they are "coached" out of their faith. Many young men have heard statements like "you gotta work hard, this ain't no Sunday school!" as if men who go to Sunday school are lazy and are less than real men who play football. Shame on the church for not offering more value to the youth in the form of challenge, involvement, and discipline. But also shame on the parents for devaluing the church and spiritual things and turning their children over to mentors who aren't often concerned with spiritual things. (Note that I said "often". There have been some great Christian coaches who changed lives forever, but they don't appear to be in the majority.)

The truth is, some are meant to play sports, some are meant to play in the band, some are meant to sing, some are meant to learn the dramatic arts, but how often is some activity that has nothing to do with their purpose pushed on them? What great purpose in their lives is thwarted or left in deficit because of the distraction?

One of the most common places this happens is in the realm of relationships. How many college scholarships have been blown by an engagement that picked up speed and soon sped up the wedding date, or worse, resulted in a baby before the wedding date? How many college scholarships have been missed that could have been achieved, but for the distraction of a high school relationship that was really out of season? It is a question of properly managing activities to stay on course for the intended destination.

Chapter 19

What do the Scriptures show us?

A good Biblical example of this is found in the story of King David and the first Jerusalem temple. David wanted to build the temple and developed plans to go with his intentions. However, the Lord knew the seasons better than David. The Lord refused David's offer to build the temple based on the fact that David was a man of war and the Temple should be built by a man of peace. (1st Kings 5:1-5)

In stopping David, the Lord showed the wisdom of the window of productivity. David was conquering tribes and kingdoms. David was vanquishing Israel's enemies. The spoils of these victories were pouring into the coffers of the kingdom. Furthermore, many surrounding kingdoms were offering tribute and gifts to keep themselves on David's good side and off his "short list". This created a "window" for stockpiling that was perfect to precede the building of the Temple.

David was so committed to the process that even when the Lord denied his most holy request (to build the house of God), he turned to stockpiling for it with all his energy. By the end of his reign the gold, silver, bronze and iron stockpiles were such as had not been heard of on the earth to that time.

It is important to listen to what God is telling us without being offended with His corrections. He knows the seasons better than we do. Often, we can't or won't recognize our season properly and He has to Guide us into our most favorable potentials.

Much of this window of efficiency has to do with managing activities. David and the men he surrounded himself with were men of war. They understood the processes of war. They understood the management of War, of battlefields, of men in arms. David had perception – the eyes and ears of faith – for the battlefield. To David's administration, constructing a temple would have been a serious distraction. They would never have been able to give it proper focus because men of war consider things in terms of winning and survival. Temples have very little to do with such things.

The contrast to this is Solomon and the men who were closest to him. Solomon was a man of peace. He had perception for judicial, educational, artistic, constructive matters for the inside of the kingdom. He surrounded himself with men of that economy. All around him were artisans, craftsman, musicians – perfect for constructing and staffing temples, perfect for managing the internal affairs of the Kingdom. These men would consider such projects, first because they could, and second because as men of peace they would make this their great contribution to the world.

Efficiency is very connected to focus. To determine if we are making the most efficient use of our season, we really evaluate our focus. Asking the correct questions about our direction, our purpose, our assignments is how we begin to move toward efficiency.

Chapter 20

Efficiency test 1

Now or Later?

What can't be done later, except at great or prohibitive expense of capital, time and relationships? This question should help us refine our activities. This is the beginning of efficiency. Sometimes it only appears to be solving efficiency later, but it is actually the most efficient thing to be done now. Good living is prepared living, and therefore, good living is preparatory living. This question should solve major focus issues and establish a good course of pursuit.

The question that follows directly on the heels of the first one is three-fold. What is primary, secondary and ancillary? Primary things are the things that are really only available in this season. They answer the "prohibitive later" question. This is not as simple to evaluate as it may appear. "Prohibitive later" has as much to do with laying proper foundations for later opportunities, activities, and events as it does with the later activities themselves. Evaluating, identifying and embracing primary pursuits is of utmost importance. The reason I use the word "embrace" is because once we have identified these pursuits, we cannot permit distraction from their accomplishment.

Now secondary things are different. They may still be necessary but the window to pursue and achieve them is much broader and the impact they have on future success is much smaller. Are they still legitimate? Certainly. Should they still be planned into our life? Of course. But are they allowed to side track the primary pursuits? No. Why? Because many of them will become primary pursuits in a future season.

I really must again ring the romantic relationship warning bell on this topic. So many times, young (and old) people give romantic relationships and marriage a "do or die" emergency level of priority. What they don't realize is if they are patient and accomplish the primary pursuits of education and career choice, of character development and personal wholeness, they become what I call "clearly defined entities". This changes the season and allows marriage to become a primary pursuit. Now romance can be built on the foundation of "this is who I am and what I do," which will draw people who have like interests to them. Rather than experiencing a life full of frustrating distraction, they will experience a life-long partnership in love and primary pursuits.

Ancillary pursuits need to be defined before we discuss them. They are the things that are legitimate, probably have some intrinsic value and yet are not necessary. Most often these are recreations and too often they compete with the primary and secondary things for valuable resources (mostly time and capital).

If they are in our life for the proper purpose of "re-creating" us, they will be beneficial. A round of golf or basketball or tennis, a Saturday in the deer-stand or in the boat, an evening at the comedy club or dinner theatre, to relieve stress and tension may actually be saving the participants from an ulcer. But when these things are elevated to the same priority as church, business, divine assignments, relationships, we are in danger of losing the preparation, investment, information and harvest of our season. A clear example is fishing. It can be used as an opportunity for family fun and fellowship or as an escape from family responsibility.

This is where we must choose between "good, better, and best." Choosing "good" is simple enough, we choose what is not "bad". It costs nothing because it saves us from the deficits of "Bad". Choosing what is "Better" costs us a little in terms of removing distractions, some of which are good. Choosing "Best" comes with a high price because we will let go of many good things and some of the better things to access the "Best" things.

Chapter 21

Efficiency test 2

What's the Point?

The next question to ask is, "What is unconnected to who I am and where I am going?" Often, we get involved in activities for the sake of others when the activity has no connection in aptitude, interest or value to us. This is not to say that some relationships aren't worth the adventure of new things, on the contrary, relationships with children often require it. Guaranteed, marriage will require it. But there is this clamoring to be accepted and included that leads many young people and adults into traps of distraction that are very detrimental. This is due to what I call "social vacuums" (insecurities) within a person that cause them to be drawn off balance in a social situation and into behavior or activities in which they would not otherwise engage. Often, something vital is set aside, or procrastinated, for something that borders on inanity. The activities and pursuits may not be bad in themselves, but they are so pointless that they represent a serious loss of resources, and really a side-track to a particular person's life. These are the things that we should label as unconnected to us and do our best to not engage in them.

This process requires emotional strength and confidence. It is a major mark of maturity. It demonstrates that a person has accepted him/her-self as God created them to be and that their goals, dreams, aptitudes and actions are valuable. It is a real sign of humility and honesty when a person puts aside the pride that is driving them to places that would side-track them and courteously declines to be involved, on the basis of other goals and dreams, and their priorities.

Maybe, a train story will best illustrate this. When I was 10 years old, my family took a vacation to Chapleau, Ontario, Canada. We spent a week at a small resort/camp on the shores of beautiful and enchanting Lake Windemere. The trip to town took about 40 minutes by dirt roads but only 15 minutes by train. The passenger train was a two-car outfit that probably held 100 people full – and it wasn't.

Most of us thought it would be wonderful to ride the train, so dad agreed to take the van into town and pick us up. He left about the same time we did, and we expected to beat him into town, but the train had travelled only a short distance when it pulled back onto the siding and sat. We sat on that siding for 20-30 minutes. Finally, a Canadian Pacific Freight came roaring by at 60 miles per hour and 200 cars long. Someone's indecision, someone's delay on that siding, had thrown us off schedule until it was no longer safe to proceed. Our window to make it into town had been compromised.

Often people allow themselves to be drawn onto some siding along the main track of their lives, and then find the window of time and capital they lost there, to have been most expensive. This leads us to the final efficiency test.

Chapter 22

Efficiency test 3

Life or Death?

There is a final question that is even more important to the efficiency issues of purpose and focus. "What is counter-productive to who I am and where I am going?" This is the question that can save us from ruin. The unconnected things distract us, but the counter-productive things disqualify and prevent us. These are the things that actually take us in the opposite direction of our purpose and assignments. This is where mistakes become catastrophic. This is where so-called friends turn out to be enemies. Dr. Mike Murdock[4] says, "An enemy is anyone who will not save you from what will destroy you." It is a colossal statement. Never let someone else's need for verification suck you into the vacuum created by their lack of character and restraint. Friends don't ask friends to ride with a drunk, a bully, a careless fool, etc . . .

Why title this chapter "Life or Death"? Isn't that exaggerating a little bit? Let's look at another Scripture from the book of Proverbs, the great wisdom treasure of King Solomon. **Proverbs 13:20** says, "He who walks with wise men will be wise, But the companion of fools will be destroyed." This scripture does not say the person is a fool, it only calls him the companion of fools, but his end is just the same. You don't have to drive drunk to be killed. You only have to be close enough to someone who is. The activities of fools are counter-productive, and actually very dangerous to us.

Physical death isn't the only death we die. There is the death of our dreams and the life God planned for us. Solomon addresses counter-productive activities in other proverbs like **Proverbs 14:1** which states, "The wise woman builds her house, But the foolish pulls it down with her hands." **Proverbs 19:1** warns, "Better to dwell in the wilderness, than with a contentious and angry woman." These passages show us a woman ruining her marriage and her household.

Consider **Proverbs 22:3** which explains, "A prudent man foresees evil and hides himself, But the simple pass on and are punished." And **Proverbs 23:21** that reveals, "the drunkard and the glutton will come to poverty. . ." There are two particularly pointed statements made in **Proverbs 6:31-32**, "when he [the thief] is found, he must restore sevenfold; He may have to give up all the substance of his house. [32]Whoever commits adultery with a woman lacks understanding; He who does so destroys his own soul."

The foolish do things that destroy their existence. Substance abuse, adultery, angry outbursts, continual contentions, these are all counter-productive behaviors and there are so many more. Anything that takes you in the opposite way of, or jeopardizes your access to God's assignment for you, is counter-productive and must be avoided at all costs.

Understanding Seasons of optimum efficiency is the best way to exploit our activities and to keep them from becoming meaningless and mundane. Knowing that what we are doing has purposeful implications lends much peace and satisfaction to the soul.

Segment 6

Seasons of Optimum Security

"Do your utmost to come before winter."
(2 Timothy 4: 21)

Security is always an important question. Is it safe to do what I am about to do? If not, will there be a safer season for this activity, process or project?

Chapter 23

What Is relevant?

The purpose of this book is to talk about life issues and processes. So, let's ask some pertinent questions. When is it safe to engage in the pursuit of romantic relationships? Have I waited until I am at peace with myself and my direction, or are there still wars going on inside of me that cause the distraction of survival to obscure who I really am? Is the person I am pursuing at peace with themselves? This is why it is so unadvisable to be in committed relationship with someone who is not a sound Christian. They haven't yet settled that inner war of the soul and spirit.

Are our circumstances such that we are making decisions based on escape and survival as opposed to character, direction and enjoyment? The decision to marry should never be based solely on the fact that the new circumstance will be more survivable than the current one. Am I falling in love with economic jeopardy; or am I asking the other person to? How will financial battles affect the nature and quality of communication?

What about business ventures? Have we evaluated the safety of the season as it relates to our intentions? What about the season of the person we are partnering with? Is this the safe season to begin; or do we wait a few months to create a buffer zone in which to overcome obscurity and become known? Often, we are so eager to commence what we are sure can work, that we don't evaluate which season will give the enterprise its best opportunity for survival.

I have great respect for my dad who has been in ministry most of his adult life, pastoring a church beyond his 71st birthday. Respect, however, does not exclude me from having fun with one of his unique little traits. Dad lived in Michigan most of his life. The winters here are very long and spring could never arrive fast enough to suit him. He would start talking about it in February if there was three-day thaw. He started looking for Robins in March. By the third week of March we were all praying for spring to arrive early so that he could quit raving about it. Funny . . . dad never planted the garden in March.

Dad grew up on a very successful farm and though the thought of spring was driving him (and the rest of us) half crazy, he knew that no plant would be safe sprouting in April. We have very late frosts here and sometimes late blizzards too. If a vegetable sprouts before the 15th of May, we need to have a way to cover it, as there will be killing frosts some nights. Dad could be ridiculous about the slow approach of spring, but he was deadly serious about the safety of the season. He planted a garden to harvest vegetables, not make himself feel better. One of his best quotes is, "I will never sacrifice your eternal future for my temporary gain."

On the topic of Dads, I would like to draw a stark parallel with a story I recently encountered. Often, dads give warnings about relationships, enterprises, courses of action, etc . . ., and their reasons seem to be too conservative. But I want to tell another story to help us understand why dads say some of the things they say.

I am writing these chapters of the book in Michigan's Upper Peninsula. At the moment I am sitting in a diner in the village of Grand Marais on the shores of Lake Superior. A few days ago, I toured the Great Lakes Shipwreck Museum at Whitefish Point. The stories that I read were astounding on this topic of seasons. Many of the wrecks listed were in the month of November. It is noteworthy that the first shipwreck recorded was in the month of November 1816.

By 1900, the weather was monitored, and reports were available to the mariners on the lakes. Yet in November of 1913, one storm sank at least 17 major shipping vessels (small craft unknown) with a loss of life well in excess of 250 people. The shipping industry wanted to blame the Weather Bureau, but the Bureau's reply was that the ship captains ignored the warnings based on pride and overconfidence, and the ship owners would insist that the ships sail to make money, not fully comprehending the dangers. With bodies and debris washing ashore in four of the five Great Lakes, the blame game went crazy, but the Weather Bureau stood firm on this fact: the warnings were issued, poor decision making started after that.

Mentors (dads and moms, pastors and teachers, etc . . .) Are like the Weather Bureau. They have a broader field of information to draw from due to their experience. They are often more concerned with what will be long term consequences than they are with immediate feelings or gains. Many times, heartbroken parents watch heartbreak happen as their headstrong children walk heedless into a seasonal disaster, in disregard of warnings given.

This question of seasonal security is not always about whether we do, or do not, attempt something. Often it is a matter of preparing for the particular contingencies which, of course, connects with the chapter on preparedness. It is certainly unwise to challenge a violent November blizzard on Lake Superior in a boat; a train with proper winter equipment running across the land next to the lake is not in the same danger.

Sometimes we can plan for the seasonal challenges, take precautions, chart a course to avoid the greatest dangers, adjust our expectations accordingly, and then, move ahead with reduced anxiety levels. All too often, young people (and headstrong old people) want to just say that they can handle the season without really making proper assessment and preparation. Again, all too often, disaster comes.

Chapter 24

What do the Scriptures show us?

For a biblical example of this we can refer back to the story from the previous season. In 1st Kings 5:4-5, Solomon stated that the Lord had given him "rest on every side" and therefore he "proposed to build a house for the Name of the Lord." This is significant in that Solomon is directly implying that the season of security allows him to consider such a building project. The absence of threat and war was the only condition in which it was safe to open the storehouses of David and expose the great stockpiles of wealth.

Let's look at another example from the scripture that youth are most interested in, Song of Solomon 2:10-14. In this scripture the lover declares to his beloved that the weather is finally right or safe for them to take a romantic trek into the mountains. Specifically, they had to wait for winter to pass. One need only think a moment to realize how dangerous a mountain area can be in the winter. He wanted to meet her near the cliffs and caves – not a safe place with snow and ice. He also said that the rains had passed. I have been hiking in the mountains of Colorado and will testify to the danger the rain presents when you are in those high canyons. Flashfloods are swift and dangerous in that environment. Landslides are not survivable.

Security Issues

Let's look at practical ways to avoid disasters. Proper seasonal assessment is the objective of this whole exercise and, as with the introduction, it is all about the question, "What time is it?" Properly assessing the security issues of a season seems as simple as observing the seasonal challenges and avoiding them. However, this can't be the case or nothing would get done in the world. Challenges are to be overcome; Dangers are to be avoided.

Challenge stretches, strengthens and grows us, which is good. Danger is different. Danger represents potential loss, potential harm, the risk of irreplaceables, irretrievables, risk of damage. These risks can usually be mitigated to mere challenges by properly responding to seasonal assessment.

Therefore, it is gravely important that we ask the correct questions to determine degree of danger as opposed to degree of difficulty. Often there is an overlapping grey area. Wisdom and discernment are evident when we know where to draw the line between brave and foolhardy.

Chapter 25

Security Issue 1

Dangers

First ask the question, "What are the dangers of the season?" We determine that by considering the inevitable. What about this season never changes, what are the uncontrollable constants? These will be the obstructions and obstacles if we are out of season. These can become vacuums that suck up our resources at an unacceptable attrition level.

Let's consider obstacles and obstructions. These are things that slow our progress. They are full of subtle traps that need to be negotiated with great care. The picture in my mind is of the military obstacle courses. They are full of barbed wire, low walls, mud pits and many other things that prevent a mad dash to the finish line. Every season has these kinds of obstacles. They require patience to deal with. A rush to the goal that disregards obstacles, will result in serious injury.

Here in Michigan it has almost become a joke to see how many car accidents will result from the first "below freezing" snow. The reason is simple. The snow represents an obstacle that requires more patience to negotiate. The thought in everyone's mind should be to slow down, specifically in curves, turns and downhill braking situations. Some don't, and the results are catastrophic. **Only a fool goes through a season slamming into, and being damaged by, it's obstacles.**

How does this apply to life seasons? Let's consider the goal of romance to be marriage and its particulars: a loving safe partnership in which we can experience sexual and emotional fulfillment; in which we can accomplish great things, such as child rearing and career goals; in which we can build legacies of love, joy and success. There are seasons of romance that match our seasons of life. The constants of theses seasons are the developmental stages. They are a combination of growth, information and experience. They are also the obstacles of the season and represent danger. Let's observe.

As a small child romance means very little because we are experiencing it through observation only, from a position close to it but not involved in it directly. We have almost no information about it. We have no character development and no physical development to support it. To try to experience it at any level deeper than external observation is catastrophic.

We get to our pre-adolescent years and we have little "walk and sit together" relationships where we are really only choosing proximity and we are actually much closer to the people with whom we play with Tonkas and Barbies. We have grown physically, and our character has sprouted but neither are developed to a point that will support more than proximity. We still know very little about physical romance and its particulars including its consequences. Physical growth is still an absolute obstruction to sexuality and emotional growth is still an obstacle to committed relationship. We have no business attempting to experience romance comprehensively.

We arrive at our teen season with amazing leaps of physical development and information. Puberty and "the talk" (too often replaced by "R-rated movies," internet porn, fashion and culture media, secular education's "health class") have engaged our curiosity and desires at a powerful level. We are now having physically and emotionally motivated "attraction/infatuation" relationships. However, character and life experience are still under-developed. Furthermore, we haven't settled core issues of life direction and competence which directly affect necessities like income. We are no longer physically obstructed but there are still definite obstacles. We still have no business plunging into comprehensive romantic involvement.

Jump ahead to college, third or fourth year. We should be very confident of our life direction, have tested our character in many stressful situations, have some definitive accomplishments behind us. Also, we should have a more comprehensive understanding of people, what we like and dislike about them, who is trying to scam us and who isn't. If we have successfully negotiated the obstacles of each season, we should be a well-defined person at this point and we should be looking for a well-defined person. At this point, a short season of real, deep investigation of character, direction and competence should qualify us to pursue a romantic relationship to its ultimate goal: Marriage with its previously mentioned particulars.

Notice how every season has obstacles. It takes very little thought to see that smashing into the obstacles would be very damaging and eventually prohibitive to the original goal or "best scenario" picture. The numbers and stories of people deeply damaged by sexual events in their childhood are a stark warning to us. The statistics on teenage pregnancy and sexually transmitted diseases, (not to mention the untold stories of emotional and physical damage experienced and caused by underdeveloped people engaging in behavior for which they haven't qualified), shout the warning again with an anguished cry.

The obstacles define the security issues, the potential for damage. Specifically, the obstructions and obstacles tell us what we cannot safely do during a specific season.

I have presented this in the context of Romantic relationships so that we grasp the picture, but the principles apply to anything from business to boating, from fishing to flying, from music to money. Ignoring them will cost us greatly in the realm of resources and may obstruct our resources all together. Not only do we lose resources of time, genius and capital when we smash into these things, they also take us way off course. That is as dangerous as any of the expenditures because, quoting Robert Frost, "Way leads on to way" and it is doubtful that we "ever return." **This is one of the biggest security issues in being out of season: going off course in an effort to compensate for uncontrollable** constants **(review chapter 11).** This is the deceptive nature of obstacles; eventually, they turn into obstructions.

Obstructions are more grave than obstacles because they represent a complete cessation of progress until they are removed. Obstructions represent catastrophic damage if we collide with them. They stand in their place with the potential for total loss. Let me demonstrate this with climate. Here in Michigan and really any location north of the 45th Parallel (half way between the Equator and the North Pole) winter is an obstruction for 4 months of the year (6 months in points north of the ¾ line). If you do not find a way to remove its threat, it will kill you.

An obstacle has become an obstruction when our goal has changed from success to survival. This is the sad saga of "out of wedlock sexuality," "out of season marriage" and "out of control divorce" in western culture. The perpetrators and their victims end up fighting for survival instead of success. Because of the emotional carnage in each situation, they stay in the survival mode rather than the success mode in the realm of relationships and sexuality and perpetuate a vicious cycle of out of season behavior. Obstructions, if not discerned and assessed can turn into vacuums.

Vacuums are just as dangerous as obstacles and obstructions because they represent meaninglessness. This is where there is a loss of any sense of original purpose and motions are performed for their own sake instead of their profitability. This is as deceptive as obstacles taking us off course, except that here we have every appearance of being on course by our activity, but the season is wrong and therefore all of our performance is really empty. No purpose. No dreams. No goals.

There are more specific things to say of these vacuums. Temptations are vacuums. They promise us satisfaction but only deliver pleasurable occurrences that are temporary. The information they give us tells us what we desire, but leaves us at the mercy of perpetual demand, because no event is adequate to satisfy us, within itself. Our temptations only create vacuums that suck us in because there are missing elements of relationship, season, and purpose.

Chapter 26

Security Issue 2

Challenges

The flip-side to Dangers is what these obstacles and obstructions become when we are in season and this brings us to the second question we need to ask, "What are the **Challenges** of this particular season?" The challenges of the security issues of any season are wrapped up in favorability. Better stated: how do we turn obstructions, obstacles, and vacuums to our favor?

Let's take the obstructions and view them through the lens of proper seasonal assessment. Here we find our obstructions have turned into anchor points. If we are in season, the uncontrollable constants are our anchor points. Anchor points are positions from which we can't fall. Anchor points represent beneficial minimums. It's OK to have your back against the wall if your enemy is stuck on the other side of it.

As a Danger, the obstacles of growth and development in the last chapter told us what we could not safely do. As **Challenges** they also tell us what we must do. This is how being excluded from something in a season actually challenges us to our more productive activities. Now we know what to focus on and, if we accept the exclusions, can focus on. Let's return to the Pikes Peak example. The mountains can't be moved, so it must be exploited as it is. The Hotel at the bottom allows it to be viewed for its Grandeur; the railway gives us access to the contours of its assent and the restaurant on the top gives us a place to look out across hundreds of miles of the country and compose our thoughts into something meaningful like "America the Beautiful" as Katherine Lee Bates did.

The obstructions out of season become observation points in season. Standing on top of these promontories allows us to see far into the distance where our goals and dreams are promising fulfillment. From here we find our landmarks that will be morale building, lifesaving reference points, as we overcome our challenges on the journey to our destiny.

How do they change so positively? When a young person asks "why" they should be willing to listen to the answer, they should be determined to get the answer that helps them, and they should be willing to embrace that answer. Yes, that is a bit of a climb up from the prideful, selfish land of "I want to do it or have it now" to the perspective-changing height of "give me information that helps me get the most out of life," but it **is** a worthwhile expedition. Those who make it will have the opportunity to see the exponentially greater good for them that awaits in a future season. (This book is dedicated to answering the question "why should or shouldn't I do a certain thing at a certain time" and it is the author's specific hope that you will embrace its information.)

Consider one of my personal experiences here. My son has his private pilot's license and can fly small airplanes. I have ridden in the airplanes with him. I like it and I want to fly, but I don't qualify. So, I inquired as to the qualifications by watching the "King Schools" ground-school DVDs. There I learned that small airplanes can go 2, 3, even 4 times faster than a car travels. Jets can fly 8 or 9 times faster than a car can travel. I also learned that they operate on a whole different set of laws than do cars. I learned that while there are greater benefits, there are also much greater dangers and that I must qualify before it is safe for me to fly. If, in a fit of selfish pride, I refuse to be instructed and go attempt to fly "out of season" I will very likely damage the plane, myself and potentially other people.

Obstacles also change by coming into proper season. These we discover have become stepping stones; launch points to the opportunities that await us. These stepping stones elevate us above the things that would pull us in, mire us, sweep over us and eventually sweep us away. It is from the elevated position atop our stepping stones that we can see our next opportunity, the next place we should step for progress toward our dreams. These launch points give us access to the opportunities of the season by keeping us on course. These launch points grant us entrance into those opportunities because we aren't so busy fighting for survival that we can't pause to redirect into a beneficial circumstance.

Vacuums also change when the seasons change. What is meaningless in one season becomes paramount experience in the next. Baby-sitting your siblings for mom or the neighbor's kids for money can seem like a pointless tedium, but when the season changes, you are married, and the children are your own, child care and the knowledge of it becomes high priority and high fulfillment.

Walking back through the scenario presented in the previous chapter is beneficial here. Sexual events that are very damaging to children and can in no way be properly called pleasurable, develop into pleasurable yet still damaging experiences after puberty, and finally change into comprehensively pleasurable and beneficial experiences when contained within a loving marriage covenant. What can only be a tragic vacuum with deceptive meaninglessness out of season, and out of boundary, becomes a pinnacle celebration of the greatest human connection God has allowed us, as we engage in them within proper season and boundary.

It is amazing how simple this process can be if everything is done in proper order, if the prohibitions of obstacles and obstructions are understood and accepted, if we avoid the deceptions of the vacuums in our lives. Suddenly, what was a real danger to us becomes some of our greatest motivators. Suddenly, the danger becomes just a challenge to be met and conquered. Through wisdom, we understand what the obstacles bar us from and what they point us to. Therein lays a subtle challenge, getting the correct information so that we get things in their proper order and employ ourselves in the correct activities.

Chapter 27

Security Issue 3

Information Sources

All great accomplishments, including the accomplishment of living the life we were designed by God to live at its maximum level, require information, or as the Military calls it, "intelligence". One of the greatest security issues we will ever encounter in properly processing our seasons, in establishing our boundaries, in living our protocol, is our sources of information.

In all things military, the source of the information must be considered as part of the intelligence gathering process to establish any sense of accuracy. And the comprehensive weight of the intelligence is often the difference between success and failure of the mission, between acceptable and unacceptable losses and between life and death. The truth is, this is also the case in life, and its various excursions.

There are several sources of life information: mentors, teachers, comrades, enemies. Each has specific information and, though they occasionally overlap in the information they give us, we need to recognize the source, and its purpose. This is the only way to properly process and respond to the information, and its source. Exploring each source, should bring clarity to why.

Mentors are one of the most important information sources because their purpose is to help us succeed comprehensively. The highest level of mentor is the person who is devoted to us succeeding at life. These mentors always try to get us this kind of "succeeding at life" information. Even though some information will seem trivial, it is targeted the same.

This level of mentorship is so important to us that God assigns us two at birth - our parents. Sometimes they fail at one particular or another, and we will need to recover in that area. Sometimes they fail comprehensively, and we must go in search of another mentor to help us (often a Pastor, or much older person with very long-range perspective). Our parents are not an excuse for our failures. This is the 21st century and there is available to us too much good information given by good people for us to blame our failures on someone else. This highest level of mentor, and parents specifically, are long term assignments from God; their word should carry tremendous weight with us. Their information should always be connected to our whole life.

There are other mentors that help us with particular seasons or areas of our life. Someone may mentor you through your college experience, or maybe through your high school sports career. Their information is going to be relevant to that season only. It will be our own deep consideration and the input of the higher level of mentors that helps us grasp that information's impact on other seasons as well. This will, by necessity, take away some of the weight of this level of mentor.

The lowest level of mentor is the person who has already succeeded at some particular objective. This may be the person who knows how to win a championship in one season, or how to succeed in Ms. Participle's English class. Their information is going to be relevant only to that particular objective. This mentor is partly in the grey area of "teacher" and points us to teachers as our next source of information.

Teachers as a source of information are often confused with mentors because much of the information given seems the same. However, the target is very different.

A teacher's job is not your success or failure. His job is the dispensing of information. He or she teaches you technical things. Those technical things may contribute to your success by advancing your skills level, but this is not mentorship and it shouldn't be. **Because teachers help in technical problem solving, to ask them to do comprehensive problem solving is to take them out of their intended task** and to put them in a place in your life to which they have not been called. They should have the good sense to stop you from placing them there. And you absolutely must have the emotional fortitude to demand that they contribute at their level only. That means that some liberal professor or school teacher has no business mentoring you. Learn your technical data and leave.

Now, the next source of information is totally different. These are our peers. **Peers give us information about what is current.** We can observe them and see the trends, the unfolding pop-culture. It is important to note that often they do not help us do the right thing with the information – they may not be doing the right thing with it themselves.

And there is more than one kind of peer in our sphere of encounters. There are **Casuals**. They don't mean us any harm with their information, they only share it incidentally as points of conversation in our brief encounter with them. Our exchange with them sounds like this,

"Those are cool pants where did you get them?"

"J. C. Penny, 30% Off."

"Thanks."

There are **Comrades**. They are in the trench with us, they have some of the same goals as we do (certainly the same goal for survival). They give us information that can be very helpful to us in warning us about what is current as a mutual participant. Our exchange sounds different:

"Dude, don't drink the prom punch."

"Why not?"

"Larry did and last time I saw him he was doing Russian squat kicks in the locker room shower . . . in a skirt."

"Thanks, I'll stick with pink lemonade."

The comrade is a unique gift from God. They are usually team-mates in one of the great enterprises of our lives. They are often as committed to our success as we are and are willing to lay down their life for us. When you have proven and qualified these, be very careful about flippantly disconnecting from them. The scripture instructs us to not forsake our friends; in the day of calamity it is better to have a friend close by than a brother way off.

This certainly was the case of David and Jonathan in 1st Samuel 18-23. Jonathan saved David's life on more than one occasion when King Saul was plotting to have David killed. The modern example is portrayed in the vivid documentation of Easy Company in World War II. Stephen Ambrose uncovered what the men thought and said of one another in interviews for his battlefield history called "Band of Brothers." It is the consensus of all who have lived through combat and of all who write about it, that the bond formed between comrades on the battlefield is unique in this world.

And, there are Enemies. These gather and share information with the intent of damaging us. They may present themselves as any one of the above sources. They are grave imposters. Some of the smoothest talkers on earth have been some of the most conscienceless villains. An enemy posing as a mentor or teacher can sound so right. An enemy posing as a comrade can appear to be interested in our welfare and benefit. But they are discovered by their core intent. They want us on their side, in their mess, profiting them, or they want us destroyed. Listen very cautiously to what they say, there is usually some hint as to their core intent. They never share information with good intent. They never glean information with good intent. They are the people who will not save you from that which will harm you.

Enemies are sources of information in a very converse way. They give us information about our weaknesses. They give us information about the contrast between what is good for us if we are patient, and bad for us if we want immediate gratification. They identify the prize by surrounding it and attempting to keep us from acquiring it. Their information is all designed to convince us that our prize is not worth the effort needed to overcome them and take it.

Most people run from enemies because it is the natural and immediate reaction to threat and resistance. But the rewards of accomplishment begin to multiply when we learn to study our enemies and then advance on them. There is recognition after defeating an enemy. There is often promotion on the other side of that recognition. There are also exponential gains once the enemy is defeated or in retreat. Even greater than gains and recognition is the idea of reputation that comes with defeating an enemy, because other enemies become hesitant to engage us and will often retreat from our subsequent objectives. Defeating enemies changes us because in the process we learn so much about ourselves and we can take that information into the calculations of soul that produce consistent success.

Information sources with all of their complexities are so important to understanding our season and the security issues in it. And we will talk more of them in the next book: "Boundaries".

Chapter 28

What time is it really . . . for you?

So as this writing draws to conclusion, only one question is paramount, and some sub-questions will help us answer this. WHAT TIME IS IT FOR YOU??!!?

What time is it inside your spirit man right now? What time is it inside your soul right now? The eternal spirit that is housed in your body must be answered. Is it in relationship with The Creator right now? Is there a burning, passion that identifies The Creator's assignment for it? What time is it right now in your soul – your mind, will and emotions – that is the bridge between your spirit-man and your body?

Yes, this is like a review of the first couple chapters but that is where it all is going to start and stop. There are some seasons that may no longer be optimum for you for various external reasons. They may have the appearance of having passed you by on society and cultural calculation of normal, but it may very well be that you are finally in a condition of spirit, a condition of soul, that makes up for external optimums. Some examples:

My own mother had once felt a pull toward nursing but then 5 babies came in a six-year span and 2 more came a few years later and what was to be done except raise the kids and help my father, the preacher, build the church. However, when the two youngest were finally both in school all day, she had the time - at 45 years old - to go back and begin taking nursing school prerequisites at the local community college.

She had never taken high school chemistry and now had to take a college chemistry course, but she also had some teenagers and college students among her older children from which to get assistance. She graduated with honors 3 years later (age 48) from that community college's nursing program and went on to practice nursing until she was 76 years old! She made her greatest salaries in the last 10 years of her career. Point? The time was right in her soul and the time was right in her house, all other factors became non-factors and the God-assignment that burned in her came to fruition!!

Another example? I have a couple in my congregation who are now retired, the wife in her mid-60's, the husband over 70, and they have adopted 2 inner-city brothers that are just entering their teen years. They have taken them from a dreadful situation with so little hope and put them in a rural school around a slower paced, much more positively influenced environment and the boys have flourished. The state did not want them to adopt because they, as a couple, were too old, not in good enough health etc . . . but we prayed, and they declared it was the right time to do the right thing and the right thing got done!!! It is quite interesting to me because these boys know how to garden, know how to come to church and sit respectfully. They are really above average for teenagers in any demographic, except the one that remains un-researched - "well raised!"

What about the rodeo cowboy in Texas who decided in his late 20's to join the Navy Seals and passed when much younger men were failing and dropping out. His name was Chris Kyle and he became the Seal's sniper known as "The Legend". What about the teenage girl who heard that there wasn't enough money to purchase all the wreaths necessary to properly place at the cemeteries of soldiers, so she started a fundraising campaign that brought in over $80,000. What about some that you know personally who came to a point of soul and Spirit and with dogged determination overcame the odds of season's long past, or way before optimum, and did great things.

In this writing we have mentioned in some detail the Biblical histories of David and Moses, both stark contrasts and yet very instructional to us in this closing theme. David was in his early teens when he killed a lion and a bear. It had nothing to do with his physical maturity, it had to with the superior condition of his soul and his faith!! He was somewhere near 17 when he killed Goliath in front of two opposing and completely astounded armies!! Yet 13 years of learning to work with other men were required before he was moved by God to the throne of Israel as their greatest warrior king! The Moses story is so different because he is 80 years old when the spiritual awakening happens for him and he leaves sheep herding in the wilderness to become the Old Testament's greatest leader/writer/miracle worker.

What time is it inside of you is the greatest question and must be answered as you finish this reading. Some of you are using the phrase "it's now or never" to excuse making another bad decision that you have no soul or spiritual preparation to apply! Some of you are trying to leap to the "prime-time" when you have invested no "prep-time"! Some of you have never admitted to yourself or your Creator that you are the one who needs healing/fixing; and another job, or spouse, or car, or dog, or whatever . . . IS NOT GOING TO FIX YOU!! You must open your eyes to the expediency of the season of your spirit and soul so that you can actually see what the season is in your environment.

Then there are some reading this who have been so long in a condition of "inadequate" and "under the circumstances and under the weather and under the critical voices and etc . . ." that you haven't opened your eyes to the set-up that God has been building around you. While you have thought that you were pining away with gifts wasted and the calendar flipping off the days/weeks/years, God has been building a team and connecting you with relationships and uncovering your strengths to others and you are now in position with the right people to go after your assignment!! For some of you it's time to not let another day pass without writing down the plan, or taking out the plan that has been written for years, and beginning to execute steps 1, 2, 3, etc . . .

Go back and review this book: what part made you burn inside with remorse, with passion, maybe with anger toward me, the writer, that I would have the gall to address your private iniquity, maybe with revelation of a missing piece, a missed consideration? What here gave you that . . . pause? The clock of God the Father, His Son Jesus, and their flowing HOLY SPIRIT, is ringing out to you right now SOMETHING!!! For their sake, for your own sake, for the sake of all who are connected to whoever and whatever God designed you to be, HEAR IT!!

I do know what time it is!! I can say with absolute certainty that it is time for you to get the past cleared up, cleared away, processed and in many cases left behind, so that you can realize that specter of the future, who seems to be so dangerously laden with the consequences of your past, can be replaced with The Creator of your life and purpose, wonderfully laden with all of His promises for your life and the living of it with purpose, passion and joy!! He wants to be both, the sweet singing angel to put you to sleep with knowledge of the day well invested and the strong, beckoning Shepherd of your dreams welcoming you to master the challenges of your tomorrows!!

Epilogue

Writing this book has been an amazing experience for me. I have very little fear about public speaking, but sitting here putting this all together, praying and pondering over the content and flow, hoping it will impact people that I cannot interact with as they encounter it, is rather daunting. When I am speaking, I can see reactions and accommodate them. Here, I have said what I have said. May it benefit the reader by confirming tough decisions, by rescinding rash ones and by engaging the mind in two and three-tiered thinking.

The seasons of our lives are so important and while I have touched some of the more abstract concepts related to them, I know that I have really only opened the topic for a new level of consideration. Don't just revisit this book for its specific topics; revisit it for how it illuminates the whole field of ideas associated with seasons. It is that visit that will benefit you the most.

Notes

1) *Sergeant York.* Howard Hawks. Hollywood, CA: Warner Brothers, 1941

2) *The Music Man.* Morton DeCosta. Hollywood, CA: Warner Brothers, 1962

3) Peter Daniels. Motivational Speaker. Quoted from various speaking events

4) Dr. Mike Murdock. Motivational Speaker. Quoted from various speaking events and religious broadcasting

5) *New King James Version*, Thomas Nelson Publishers, 1997